W9-BRT-355

RESCUING JULIA TWICE

MORE PRAISE FOR *RESCUING JULIA TWICE*

"Tina Traster deftly tells of the slow dawning that things aren't quite right between her and her baby daughter. How Tina uncovers what had been concealed from her and turns around a devastating diagnosis is nothing short of stunning. This book will stay with you long after you close the cover."

—Lori Holden, author of *The Open-Hearted Way to Open Adoption*

"I am in awe of Tina and her husband, and the wonderful success they have had with Julia. If you are an adoptive parent, don't miss this book."

—Jane Ballback, executive editor, *Adoption Voices*

"Traster's experiences and the way she writes about the realities of adoption are very helpful to everyone raising a child with RAD or thinking of adopting a child who may have RAD."

—Irene Clements, president, National Foster Parent Association

"Tina's journey hit very close to home. I know it will offer understanding for those finding themselves on a similar path with adopted children they're helping to heal and love."

—Tiffany Sudela-Junker, producer and director, *My Name Is Faith*

"Having raised three kids with varying degrees of RAD, I know how much this book is needed!"

—Julie Valentine, editor, adopting.com

Rescuing Julia Twice

A Mother's Tale of Russian Adoption and Overcoming Reactive Attachment Disorder

Tina Traster

Foreword by Melissa Fay Greene

Published by Chicago Review Press, Incorporated
814 North Franklin Street
Chicago, Illinois 60610

ISBN 978-1-61374-678-3

Library of Congress Cataloging-in-Publication Data

Traster, Tina.
Rescuing Julia twice : a mother's tale of Russian adoption and overcoming reactive attachment disorder / Tina Traster ; foreword by Melissa Fay Greene.
pages cm
Includes index.
ISBN 978-1-61374-678-3 (cloth)
1. Attachment disorder in children. 2. Adoptive parents—United States—Biography. 3. Intercountry adoption—Russia (Federation) 4. Intercountry adoption—United States. 5. Adopted children—Family relationships—United States. I. Title.

RJ507.A77T73 2014
618.92'85880092—dc23
[B]

2013039314

Interior design: Sarah Olson

http://juliaandme.com

Printed in the United States of America
5 4 3 2 1

This book is dedicated to Julia Sophie Tannenbaum, my daughter, my inspiration, my beacon. Our journey together has taught me to live life more patiently, to embrace challenges of the heart with fortitude, to welcome imperfect love with grace and acceptance.

Contents

Foreword

Every dream of adoption—like every fantasy about parenthood—is really a dream of attachment. Whether or not a person ever uses the word *attachment* (the word was coined in the 1960s by the great twentieth-century British psychiatrist John Bowlby), a prospective mother or father surely envisions rocking a baby in a soft-lit nursery; running behind a tiny two-wheeler powered by a ferocious, chubby-legged piston; or slow-tossing a Wiffle ball toward a smudged little face all but hidden under a baseball cap. No one thinks attachment. It goes without saying that each imagined scene is knit together by empathy and love, eye contact and merriment, intimacy and laughter. You no more dream about attachment than you head to a clothing store with thoughts of well-made stitches and seams. And if all goes well with a baby—if he or she is born healthy and enjoys tender, attentive nurturing from the first moments of life—then the parents' handmade scrapbooks and online photo albums will swell with happiness, showering the world with glimpses of first smiles, first steps, first birthday candles, and first days of school.

Human babies are pretty resilient. The vast majority are born well-equipped with all the darling qualities that draw parents close. The vast majority are wired to fall madly in love with their cooing, looming, giant parents. It's an obvious evolutionary mechanism. But what of babies who, through no fault of their own, through congenital issues, illness, birth trauma, or socioeconomic forces that pry them from their biological parents' arms, are unable to attract permanent devoted caregivers and cannot seem to locate an adult to adore? A baby will try and try and try, but little by little—each infant is different—a touch of baby despair appears. True grief enters when a baby—say a baby abandoned to an overcrowded institution with an underpaid, rotating staff of caregivers—feels itself cast loose from humanity, sailing alone across a black Arctic sea on an ice floe beyond sight of shore.

What happens to such a baby if she is not rescued before the light in her eyes has gone out? When a baby or young child who has lost her optimism and love is finally dragged out of her bed and placed in the arms of an adoptive parent—can the sweet pas de deux begin? Not necessarily. When a baby or young child has learned that no one is coming; that no one thinks he or she is the cutest little baby on earth; that he or she must weather hunger, cold, and sickness in solitary, those are hard lessons to unlearn. It's nearly impossible to convince a child that he or she is no longer alone in the universe. When a child belatedly offered family life fiercely rejects the proposition that one or more loving adults has now arrived for good, the professionals begin to speak of attachment as in "attachment issues" or "attachment disorder."

And a new parent's dream of singing lullabies to a drowsy child, of chasing after a tiny two-wheeler while screaming encouragement, of softly tossing a Wiffle ball light as air must be postponed in deference to simpler hopes: the dream that the child will look into her parent's eyes and smile; that the distressed child will seek out the new mother or father above all others; that the hungry child will accept food from the parent; that the enraged child will allow the mother or father to help her find peace.

This is the story of one girl among millions, in whose eyes the light of hope and love and happiness faded and then flickered out. It's the story of one mother and father among millions, for whom the girl was not a throwaway, not one in a million, but the most precious of all children. Finally it's the story of how those parents dedicated their lives to rekindling the light in their daughter's eyes and how all three have been fantastically enlarged, rewarded, and enriched by the happy result.

Melissa Fay Greene is the award-winning author of five books of nonfiction, including *There Is No Me Without You: One Woman's Odyssey to Rescue Her Country's Children*, about the HIV/AIDS African orphan crisis, and *No Biking in the House Without a Helmet*, about raising her family. She and her husband are the parents of nine children—four by birth and five by adoption.

RESCUING JULIA TWICE

Prologue

Angelina Jolie and Brad Pitt make it look easy. They adopt kids from all corners of the world, and the media broadcasts images of perfect Kodak moments. They'd have you believe that families bond and blend instantaneously.

They don't. Not always. Not in my experience or in the experience of many others. Sometimes the road to loving your adopted child is long and twisted and scary. You know something is wrong—but is it the child? Is it you? You drown in shame and confusion, hiding your feelings from the world. It can't possibly be that you've gone to the other end of the world to get this baby and you're not bonded after a month, six months, two years.

I knew something wasn't right early on. We adopted Julia from a Siberian orphanage in February 2003. She didn't clutch to me nor gaze in my eyes. She never rested her head on my shoulder or relaxed into a warm embrace. She didn't respond if I sang or read to her. It was like she was there but wasn't.

For a while, weeks, maybe months, I sank deeper and deeper into depression, thinking I'd made a terrible mistake. Maybe I wasn't cut out to be a mother.

Julia was a little more responsive with my husband but only somewhat. For the first ten months, I suffered guilt, shame, and sadness. After traveling ten thousand miles (twice) to bring home this child, I was unwilling to let anyone know how I really felt. Then the revelations began. I hired a daytime nanny in early 2004. Anna was twenty-one, experienced and energetic. She'd come with a glowing review from the mother of her last charges. When she mentioned Julia was having trouble warming up to her, a ding went off in my head. Why? Why isn't Julia connecting to this lovely young lady who took her daily to the park, to play dates, to "mommy and me" classes? I had thought for sure that Anna might be able to give her what I couldn't.

A year later, I enrolled Julia in preschool and saw more of the same: a child who was not bonding with teachers or other children. She was as much an enigma to others as she was to us. Everyone agreed she was gregarious, vivacious, friendly, and outgoing. Yet at the same time, she was aloof, hard to figure out. When I picked her up at the end of the day, she was always by herself, sometimes sitting under a desk. Worried, I mentioned her odd behavior to her pediatrician. That was the first time I took notice of the phrase "Reactive Attachment Disorder" (RAD), even though I had heard it mentioned before. The doctor, who worked with foreign adoptees, explained RAD was common among institutionalized children. The early break from birth mothers causes trauma that makes it difficult for the child to trust or attach to another adult. This, he explained, is why Julia recoils when she is held. Why she doesn't have a favorite teddy. Why she won't make eye contact.

I wasn't ready to hear this. I told myself we just needed more time. I stored the doctor's explanation in the back of my mind, but pieces of it drifted out when I watched Julia fight naps or wander away from me constantly. Finally, when she was four, I was ready to face her demons, our demons. It was during a nursery school recital that I broke down and sobbed because I realized how lonely, displaced, and isolated my daughter was. Julia was unable to sing along with the group. Her disruptive behavior forced a teacher to take her off the stage and leave the room. This may not sound like the most unusual event for a young child—but put in context, I understood right then and there that I needed to intervene.

My husband, Ricky, and I banded together to read everything we could on the syndrome. We made a dogged effort and a conscious commitment to help our daughter and make ourselves into a family. It was our daily work. We learned that raising a child who has trouble bonding requires counterintuitive parenting techniques—some that disturbed and surprised family and friends. People could not understand when we'd respond to Julia's fussing with a passive poker face rather than indulge her. We'd laugh during her tantrums until she abandoned them and moved on as though they'd never happened. They didn't understand that Julia wasn't willing to give hugs, and we didn't ask her to do so. With the help of research and case studies, we had a toolbox. Some advice was invaluable; some failed. Some techniques worked for a while. We were living inside a laboratory. I knew how lucky I was to have a partner like Ricky, because so many marriages and homes are ravaged by the challenge of adopting difficult children.

Over time, there was more engagement with Julia. It wasn't necessarily loving and warm at first, but it moved in the right direction. We were drawing her out. She became more capable of showing anger rather than indifference. As her verbal skills developed, we had the advantage of being able to explain to her that we loved her and would never leave her. That we understood how scary it was for her to be loved by an adult and that she was safe.

Progress took time, and the work of staying bonded with a wounded child is a lifetime endeavor. That's okay though, because Julia has stepped out of the danger zone. She's taken off her helmet and armor. She has let me become her mother. And I honor that trust by remembering, each and every day, how she struggles with subconscious demons and how mighty her battle is and will always be.

Author's note: Out of respect for their privacy, I have changed the names of some of the people who appear in these pages.

PART ONE

A Daughter Waiting in Siberia

One

Olga is waiting for us as we leave the baggage carousel. She is a pretty thing, with a round doll's face and Delft-blue eyes. She holds a sign with our surname, Tannenbaum. After greeting us with a firm handshake, she takes us to an airport travel agent and helps my husband and me buy tickets to Novosibirsk, Siberia's capital. We pass tired-looking soldiers in ill-fitting uniforms. Without pronouns she explains what will happen to us over the next twelve hours. But before anything happens, we go to the Novotel in Moscow's Sheremetyevo International Airport for four hours of sleep and a meal.

Olga says, "Arrive 10:00 PM. Take to Domodedovo Airport."

Olga's step-by-step instructions are a comfort; I already feel as if I have been carved out of my body. I am floating above myself, watching. Could be Sudafed's mind-altering effects; more likely it is the enormity of our journey ahead. How does one prepare to meet her daughter for the first time? At a Siberian orphanage?

∞∞∞

I don't know what time it is. It's dark. Ricky and I are lying in the warm and comfortable hotel bed, giddy and disoriented. The alarm startles us. We shower, dress, and go to the hotel lobby atrium to eat, the first decent food we've had since we left New York. Ten sharp, Olga and the driver, her husband, pull up in front of the hotel. Olga asks us about our nap and dinner in clipped English while her stoic husband grabs our suitcase. We slide into a stale, smoky van with drawn-curtain windows and begin what seems like a covert operation. We are like refugees being smuggled across an illegal border, though we haven't left Moscow yet.

Domodedovo Airport, Moscow's airport for domestic travel, is a shock—a place suspended in the mid-twentieth century with exposed steel girders and acrid smoke hanging in the air. Olga helps us check in. Everyone's eyes follow us. Even with my fur coat and my husband's Russian-style sheepskin hat, we are obvious outsiders. Men with deep fissures in their faces wear hats piled like birds' nests and carry worn briefcases. Olga tells us they're traders from the East. Some are accompanied by tall, elegant women who look like pigment-less stars from old Hollywood.

Olga leaves us, our last link to anything accessible. My stomach somersaults.

We amble into the waiting lounge, aided by our phonetic glossary of the Russian alphabet. A man is peering inside a briefcase propped on his thighs, cackling like a lunatic. With 9/11 still fresh in memory, he frightens me. No one here speaks English. I nudge my husband. "That guy doesn't seem right. We should tell someone."

Ricky glances over at him, then at the briefcase. "He's looking at an accounting ledger," he says, stroking my shoulder. "Probably laughing because he's made a lot of rubles."

Ricky and I have been together for only two years, but he knows how to diffuse my bomb. We had been childhood and college friends and reunited in romance in late 2000, when we were both thirty-eight. We married six months later and agreed we wanted a child. The fertility mill was a disaster—a large gamble with low odds—so we moved on to adoption. We chose a foreign adoption because we heard it was an easy though expensive transaction. No advertising in the *Penny Saver* papers. No birth mothers to deal with. No uncertain outcomes. Russia appealed to us because our grandparents hailed from Eastern Europe; we felt as though we were paying homage to our history by adopting from Russia.

Our flight is called. We're led outside onto the tarmac. Snow swirls. Frigid air bites at the exposed parts of my face. This can't be my life. I don't need another adventure to share with my friends and family. There are stories about older parents who are preparing to adopt a child and boom, they're pregnant. The woman always gets pregnant while she's scouting the adoption classifieds to find a young mother who needs to give up her baby. It's a nice fairy tale.

The plane is more of a relic than the airport. The windows are rusted and mismatched. There is duct tape on some. I don't want to know why. The seats are cramped. I slide into the window seat and gasp. Snow hits the window with crystal pings. The ground crew keeps deicing the wings. I can't breathe. I don't like to fly generally, but no one should fly on a night like this—not even someone who has a daughter waiting in Siberia. I want to run off this decrepit plane, but the bulkhead door has already been sealed shut.

"Do we really want a baby this badly?" I ask my husband.

He thinks I'm joking. I don't think I am. I don't know what I think except that there's a good chance we will die on this plane tonight somewhere over the Russian tundra. My mind races to CNN breaking reports about planes going down "somewhere in Russia." Pilot error. Navigators impaired by alcohol. Bum radar in the control tower.

Surprisingly, the plane lifts off the ground with the grace of a heron. My eyes are closed, and I'm clutching my husband's hand. I'm moving through the longest night of my life, moving toward something I've told myself I want, yet I feel numb. It could be my cautious nature, but I know it's not. I am making a lifetime commitment to raise a child given up by another woman. A final, irreversible decision. I worry about our financial stability, though the real fear is more primal. Something I can't articulate is keeping me up at night and giving me stomachaches. I can feel it in my bones.

I rifle through my travel bag and pull out Colin Thubron's travelogue *In Siberia*. The man has traversed the vast territory, traveling alone by train, boat, car, and on foot. I picked up the book during my last trip to Barnes & Noble. I remember thinking I should probably get one or two parenting books, but I couldn't bring myself to do so. Either I didn't believe there was a manual for raising children, or I wasn't ready to accept that I was going to become a parent. Okay, not just a parent, a *mother*. Easier, I thought, to read about this vast, mysterious place that I associate with dislocation, with lore, with *Doctor Zhivago* and *Reds*.

∞∞∞

Our adoption process had taken place in record time. Three months after completing our dossier in August 2002, we got the call. I thought it must be a mistake, but it wasn't. There was a six-month-old baby girl in Novosibirsk waiting for a home. We'd been told most adoptions take between a year and eighteen months. Also, we had requested as young a baby as possible but had been told most Russian babies are at least a year old when they leave the orphanages. My head spun when the social worker called. All those times I wanted so desperately to see the little pink plus icon on the pregnancy stick. Would I have felt just as panicked if I had? Her words seemed surreal: *We've got a baby for you.*

I thought, *This can't be. It's only been four months. Four months! I'm not ready. We haven't done anything to prepare for an actual baby—only for the idea of having a baby.* We hadn't even decided where she was going to sleep. And I had writing deadlines. So many deadlines, so much pressure—it was hard to contemplate a disruption as big as a baby. But this was the baby I told myself I wanted so badly. We had used our life savings to make this happen. Nothing else should have mattered. But I didn't feel ecstatic.

Why?

What was wrong with me?

This queasy ambivalence was entirely in character for me. I often want something, go after it with a vengeance, and then go through a period of regret and remorse. It may be that deep down I fear commitment. I'm afraid to fail, afraid that after I get what I want, the other shoe will drop. In that moment when the social worker said, "We have a baby for you," I knew I was in troubling territory.

The quick timing threw me off-kilter. At this point adopting a baby still seemed theoretical, conceptual—something that would happen down the road. Soon after the call, we received a grainy video of a baby being coaxed to smile and crawl for the camera. She wore a diaper. She had the palest skin I'd ever seen and eyes as dark as a tree hollow. She was a piece of merchandise for sale, an object held before the camera to be marketed. I cried hard—for her abandonment, my disappointments, the way circumstance unites a mother and child.

"She looks like a fine baby to me," Ricky had said, sitting on the couch, relaxed and curious. I didn't disagree, but I didn't feel an impulse to run to the child, lift her from that dreadful place, and bring her to my breast. I simply felt sad. I let my husband's practical certainty carry me through to the next phase. We agreed to meet the child. Everything else took a backseat to preparing for our two trips to Siberia, the first one just after New Year's Eve 2003. It was necessary to use what little money we had to pay for fees and travel. My husband and I swallowed our pride and asked for financial help from family and one particular friend, Leah, who proved to be a guardian angel. We kept moving forward, one antiseptic step at a time. I went to a Russian agency for visas. I bought thermal socks and heavy boots. I organized my work so I would not miss a deadline. I walked through steps, checked off checklists. Nothing about this felt like preparation for motherhood. My belly didn't grow. There was no baby inside me.

∞∞∞

Six hours later, the plane lands at Tolmachevo Airport in Ob. We've flown through eleven time zones. It is 5:00 AM, still dark. An endless night. A steward leads us down a flight of metal steps toward the tarmac. Like everyone else, he seems to know why we are here, but how can that be? Breathing in the bracing air scorches my lungs. This is what ten degrees below zero feels like. We walk toward a hangar-style building shrouded in darkness. A loud *thunk*—bright lights illuminate the cavernous space. Most of it is filled up with a conveyor belt. Above it is a billowy soft banner that says "City of Industrial Science" in English. Below, another sign says "New York Pizza." A tall man in an army jacket holds a sign with our surname. Unlike Olga, Vladimir meets us with an expressionless nod. When I ask him to direct me to the toilet, he points blankly at a padlocked door. He lets my husband carry our suitcase. He walks in front of us to his Volga.

We slide into the backseat and sit closely together. Vladimir turns on the scratchy radio, and the guttural sounds of Russian fill the car. It is 7:00 AM, coal black outside, a continuous January night. He drives fast, swerving hard once to miss a wolfish dog that darts into the road. I notice a woman standing stoically in an eerily-lit bus shelter, her breath billowing from her hooded face.

Twenty minutes later, Vladimir pulls up in front of a squat brick building, the Centralnaya Hotel.

"Olga, meet 9:30 AM, lobby." The only words he utters, carefully memorized.

Two

The woman behind the glass partition at the Centralnaya Hotel rubs sleep from her eyes and reveals an irritated expression. "Where can we get some breakfast?" I ask. She doesn't answer. I am starving, feverish, and weak. She hands us a heavy, weighted room key. It is a jail cell, oppressively hot with windows high on the walls. They are thickly caked with ice, so encrusted that when the sun finally comes up three hours later, it looks as though the windows are opaque squares rather than transparent portals to the outside world. There's a sparse sitting room with a tiny couch and writing desk. Two threadbare cots on opposite sides of the claustrophobic room are on the other side of a thin wall. The misshapen toilet forces your skin to make contact with the bowl when you sit down. There's no shower curtain and only cold water. My husband suggests we try and find some breakfast before Olga (it seems all translators are named Olga) arrives.

Ricky and I stop at the front desk and ask where we can find a café or bakery. The same sleepy hotel clerk shrugs. As we walk outside the hotel, right across the street is the most beautiful bakery I've ever seen. It has a large glass window, steamed over from the frigid morning air, with oceans of cakes and confections. We'd been told dollars would be accepted in Russia. The woman in the tall paper baker's hat keeps waving at our currency and shaking her head. We need to exchange money but cannot find an open bank.

"I have three thousand dollars strapped to my chest, but I can't get a cup of tea," my husband says.

ᴑᴑᴑᴑᴑᴑ

We return to the hotel lobby. I alternate between sulking and fuming. Why do we have to be treated so coldly? What is wrong with these people? Why is this journey so fraught with pain? The little voice taunts: *Is it because you don't want this badly enough? Isn't a woman willing to endure anything to have her baby?*

Olga is a willowy beauty with alabaster skin and slightly slanted purplish eyes. She has a good command of English. She tells us she's lived and worked in Saudi Arabia and Switzerland. Alla is the one who makes the decisions. She is square and squat, and her cropped black hair looks as if it is pasted to her face. On the way to Vladimir's Volga, Alla fingers my mink. "Very nice," she says.

It is near ten, and the sun is finally rising. Before we enter the Ministry of Education, an imposing government building in the heart of Novosibirsk, Olga leans toward us and says, "Someone is going to ask you if you have seen your child. All you say is, 'We have not seen our child.'" Olga continues. "The ministry will tell you that they have a child for you. Act surprised." It is a charade.

ᴑᴑᴑᴑᴑᴑ

No one shows up for our appointment. Olga, who takes pity on me because I'm suffering with high fever and obvious signs of flu, escorts us to a tiny tea cart on the second floor. We buy tepid tea and stale biscuits as moist as paint chips. "Let's go to the orphanage," Olga says. "We'll come back here later."

The landscape changes dramatically as we drive away from the bustle of the city center to clusters of Soviet-era concrete buildings, linear, gray, and featureless. En route, we pass a large hospital. Olga says, "This is where your child was born." I try to imagine baby Yulia coming into a world where she is not wanted. If the information we've been given can be trusted, we know her mother is a twenty-year-old who already has two children. We know her name is Maria and that she is very short, four feet nine. She is married. We don't know the father's name. The medical records say baby Yulia spent the first three months of her life in the hospital being treated for a respiratory infection and dysentery. We don't know if this is true. Everyone tells us the medical records are a sham. They're exaggerated so the Russian government can tell the Russian people there's a good justification for "selling" babies to foreigners. It's a crazy game, but Americans adopting babies want babies so badly they play along. In Siberia, an American floats through a surreal dream-nightmare staged for her and well rehearsed by players in the baby industry.

As we get closer to the orphanage, I notice scarlet-faced men lying faceup on the side of the road. "What are they doing out there?" I ask Olga.

"They are drunk. On vodka. It is a sickness. Russia's national disease." Olga's frankness startles. Until now the conversation has been curt. She softens when she speaks about how difficult the end of communism has been for so many of those who've never known anything but a subsidized existence. She tells us Siberia has been behind the Iron Curtain for six decades, and essentially it still is. People here are wary of Westerners and of capitalism.

When Olga says this, I tell her that when we've been out on the streets alone, people have looked at us with a combination of disgust and disdain.

"That's because people in Novosibirsk know Americans are here for adoptions. To them, you're stealing their babies," she says matter-of-factly. The looks on the faces of the airplane steward, the hotel clerk, and the bakery cashier suddenly made sense to me. I was the object of their disdain. And I guess taking babies from their orphanages reminded them either of their society's failings or their fear of an open society where failure is a harsh reality.

OOOOOO

Orphanage Number Two has no sign on it. It is another one of Siberia's secrets. We slip into the dimly lit building. It is stiflingly hot. Women furiously dust and polish staircase banisters, but they don't meet our eyes when we ascend the stairs. I can't believe that babies live here—one hundred babies, ten to a room. There is life and promise, I suppose, at least for the children who are "good" enough to adopt out. We've been told many children are afflicted with fetal alcohol syndrome, a disease that causes mental problems. Those children will never leave these austere places. We're led into a large room. A group of babies are in a giant crib, like a choreographed diaper advertisement. Older toddlers zip around in mobile chairs. A caretaker changes a diaper. A couple is handed a wriggling baby. I'm still sick with flu and fever. Olga and Alla are conferencing about something that has to do with me. Olga's voice rises, and Alla eventually seems to give in to something. Then I'm led to a chair outside the baby room and handed a surgical mask. "Alla thought you were too sick to hold the baby," she says. "Wear this."

I'm sitting in the chair. Ricky is standing beside me, his hand resting on my shoulder. My eyes dart left and right, searching for the caretaker who will bring us our baby. We have decided that we will change her name from Yulia to Julia, which is our best effort at allowing her to keep the only thing she's been given: a name. But at the same time, we're Americanizing it to Julia so she will not have to explain why she has an odd name. Names shape us. When I was born in 1962, my mother had seen a French model named "Bettina" in a fashion magazine. That was what they called me when I was born, but by the time I got to second grade, kids made fun. They rhymed the name into cruel configurations. *Bettina betina, vagina.* After that, I was called Tina.

I'm scanning the room, trying to match babies' faces with the one I had seen on the tape. "Is that her?" I ask Olga.

"No, she's over there."

I'm stunned when I see the baby on the changing table. She turns her head toward me and flashes a dimpled smile. Does she instinctively know she will be mine and I will be hers? She is smaller than I imagined.

The caretaker, who has her swaddled in a blanket, says to me, "Pick up baby." I hesitate. Fear whips me with hurricane force. I can't move. Instead, the caretaker places her in my arms, where she fits exactly right. I look into her eyes. They are khaki. I touch her fuzzy bald head. Her nose is runny and red. The caretaker hands me a brown tea concoction in a bottle and says, "Feed baby." I do and then hand her to my husband. He pulls her close to his chest and says, looking down, "What's new?" I want to laugh and to cry. I want to run and to cling. I wish I could dance and spin in a sun-filled meadow with clean, bright light. In the orphanage chair, I sit still.

Time is suspended.

Everything falls away.

We have thirty minutes with the baby before she's returned to her tiny crib in the baby room. She is one of ten babies who share the room. There's a little boy in the baby room who has a large head, and his eyes are far apart. That is what fetal alcohol syndrome looks like. That little boy has no chance of being adopted. The caretaker lowers Julia into the cramped bed and tightly swaddles her, almost as though she's imprisoned. She leaves her with a half-empty bottle of the tea concoction. This tiny soul is straightjacketed into a crib where her needs will be met only when a caretaker can get around to responding. But what can they do? They have a hundred babies to care for.

Julia has a little smile on her face. I think she knows her fate will change. There is something about her dark, deep eyes that suggest she's lived on this planet more than six months. They have a knowing quality.

We next meet with the orphanage director. I ask questions about the health of the baby's mother. They are not answered. Then Vladimir drives us back to town and drops us off at the Irish grill, where we order blinis and salmon roe and shrimp kabob. We are grateful and relieved to be left alone for a couple of hours to talk about our daughter. We agree she is startlingly beautiful. We see her in the Russian faces around us—broad cheeks, slightly slanted eyes, skin like goat's milk.

ᴑᴑᴑᴑᴑᴑ

That evening we venture out on our own for dinner. Whatever sunlight we saw that day had come and gone quickly. The night air is as sharp as a cat's claws. It tears the skin.

People walking down Krasnyi Prospekt, the wide and vast main boulevard, look like floating apparitions, small and shimmery with plumes of steam trailing them. The majestically domed Opera and Ballet Theater anchors the street at one end. Siberia is otherworldly. I could not compare it to anywhere I'd been or anything I'd ever experienced. At Patio Pizza we find comfort. American-style pizzas and a waiter who is happy to practice his English. He spends a lot of time hanging around our table. He easily guesses we are adoptive parents, and I wonder if he thinks we're baby stealers. He tells us he likes to practice his English: *Do we mind if we chat?* We are delighted to do so. He's a student. He wants to study international relations. We tell him we are here to adopt a baby, and he says he already knew that. Then he pulls a pen from behind his ear and grabs an empty napkin. "What is your name?" he asks. I say "Tina." He scribbles a few letters on the napkin and then shows it to me. "Tuha. That's your name in Russian," he says, smiling.

I run my index finger over the name to make sure the ink is dry and place it into a safe compartment in my bag. I smile at this young man.

ᴑᴑᴑᴑᴑᴑ

I cannot sleep. I watch my husband sleep peacefully on the rickety cot in the stifling hot room that feels like a lockup. The room is inky dark, but I write in my journal. I wait for 7 AM before nudging Ricky from slumber. "C'mon," I say. "Let's go to the bakery across the street." Groggily he says, "It's the middle of the night. It's pitch dark." I tell him it is morning. "Remember, the sun doesn't rise until after 9." The bakery is sultry, like a Laundromat. The tea and pastries are delicious. We pay with rubles, converted from our dollars.

Olga picks us up after breakfast, and Vladimir drives to the orphanage. The sun climbs into the blue sky. But a sunny day doesn't change the dull cast or the monotony of the section of town where Orphanage Number Two is located. Again we ascend the clean steps to the waiting area outside the baby room. The ruddy-cheeked caretaker hands me Julia, who is wearing clownish pajamas and mismatched socks. Her big toe pokes through a hole in the sock on her right foot. We three are sent to a large gym where we spend time with the baby crawling around on a giant rubber mat. A few young blonde girls, aged between three and five, skip into the room singing a tune. There is a piano at that far end of the gym, but the girls only stay for a few minutes and dance around before a caretaker seems to admonish them to leave. It is impossible to know why they were never adopted. They might have been brought here when they were two or three or older, and most adoptive parents want a baby. We have been told that there are half a million children living in Russian orphanages. Those who are "unadoptable" will stay in a place like this until they turn eighteen.

∞∞∞

The next day we will leave Novosibirsk without Julia. The Russian government requires adoptive parents to make two trips. Everyone tells us we will be called back in the next three to six months. I doubt she will remember us when we see her, so I savor our last moments with her. I nuzzle my nose against her skin. She doesn't smell especially good, the way babies are supposed to smell. While sitting on the mat in the gym, I notice she is transfixed by the enormous ice-glazed windows high on the wall. I try to distract her with a big, bouncy ball, but she is craning her neck. She squints hard, staring intently at the burst of white light outside the room, a strange phenomenon. Julia has never seen daylight. The sun has never kissed her skin. She'd been transported from the hospital to the orphanage in October, when it was too cold for the babies to be taken outside.

Three

I cannot wait to escape Siberia, even though we are leaving a baby, *our baby*, behind. An American woman we met made an incisive observation about the city and the experience Americans have in it. She said, "You could take photographs in color, but when they get developed they'll be in black and white." We knew exactly what she meant. Everything about this place is harsh: the guttural sounds, the cold stares, the tight leashes adoption handlers keep Americans on. People dressed in masses of dark clothing getting where they need to go. Ammonia permeates every building, especially the tomb-like orphanage.

My fanatical desire to leave Novosibirsk comes with a feeling of remorse, too. This is, after all, Julia's place of birth. She might have grown up here. Somewhere in this city she has a mother, a father, and two siblings. Girls, I think. Maybe there are grandparents and cousins, too. We will never know. Someday we'll want to tell her about this faraway city in the geographical center of Russia. We're told it's quite beautiful here in the warm weather, though I think if we ever returned with Julia, I'd want to do so in the heart of winter because I'd like her to know that she comes from people who endure extreme hardships. There's something romantic about that history.

I'm hoping when we come back—three to six months from now—Novosibirsk may feel more welcoming. Maybe flowers will be in bloom.

When I arranged our trip to Russia, I built in a four-day diversion in Moscow.

"Why not," I'd said to Ricky. "We're already there. Besides, the next time we pass through Moscow, we'll have Julia with us, and I don't think we'll be in the mood for touring Red Square."

He agreed.

The prospect of balancing this momentous journey with pleasure brought comfort. But when I mentioned our intention to our American adoption counselor, she balked.

"Oh, no, that will not be permissible," she said.

"Not permissible? What do you mean?" I replied, thinking I must have misheard her.

"Yes, no, um, the Russian government doesn't want adoptive parents in Russia on their own," she said.

Now this was sounding farcical to me. Throughout the adoption process, we'd been shepherded through every step. In Novosibirsk our passports were kept by the hotel clerk until we left the city, and when we asked Olga why this was necessary, she shrugged. But now, being told we couldn't travel at the end of our trip, was beyond what I could tolerate.

"I'm sorry," I said. "I have made plans, and I intend to keep them."

I could imagine the counselor putting a yellow sticky on my folder that said "Difficult client" or some such label. However, for reasons I'll never understand, she backed off and said, "Okay then, do what you must."

I booked three nights at the Moscow Marriott. I'd had just about enough of feeling yoked.

Everything about the adoption process puts you under a microscope. It starts when the counselor comes to conduct the "home study," which is a vetting process that determines whether you're suitable parents and whether you can provide a safe, loving home. Really, it's a sham, though it still feels invasive when a stranger steps into your apartment and asks you where the baby is going to sleep and what kind of a relationship you have with your mother. The counselor is clearly ticking off questions from a checklist, but there is nothing about this interchange that feels genuine. As long as I give her the right answers, she's satisfied. Then there are the fingerprints at the police station to prove you're not a convicted felon or a child molester. And the financial disclosures and letters of recommendations and health declarations.

Why isn't every parent subjected to all this? Come to think of it, maybe that doesn't seem like a bad idea.

The Marriott Hotel on Tverskaya Street seems like a gleaming palace after doing time at the Centralnaya Hotel in Novosibirsk. There are marble floors and human-size elevators and obliging concierges who are only too happy to arrange tickets to the Bolshoi Ballet or make a dinner reservation. After arriving at our room, I stand in the shower for twenty minutes, washing away days of discomfort and compromised bathing. I rotate my neck and let hot water penetrate into my shoulders. I stay in the shower until I'm light-headed from the heat and steam. Everything about the heat and the lovely little complimentary shampoos and the marble tiles distances me from where we've been. Because I like to think in metaphors, I picture Novosibirsk as a labor pain. Birth mothers, of course, must go through excruciating pain to have a child. Is this process my equivalent? The pain I must experience to know joy?

Right now, though, I don't want to think about Novosibirsk or Olga or ammonia-scented orphanages or the fact that we're going to have to come back and do this all over before we can bring Julia home. Right now I want to be a tourist. I want to read about Russia in the travel books I've brought on the trip and plan our days ahead.

Ricky and I dress for dinner. It's still necessary to wear layers because Moscow is cold, too. It's about zero degrees, maybe ten degrees warmer than Siberia. Ricky is wearing lined cargo pants, a turtleneck, and a black sweater. He looks handsome tonight. I have put on a dab of makeup for the first time in forever, though I still feel laden because I'm wearing long underwear under my pants and three layers of wool on top.

We put on our coats, hats, and gloves, and the concierge hails us a cab to take us just a few blocks to the restaurant. It is snowing.

It is a trendy place, large and angular with abstract art on the walls and candlelit tables.

"This is a step up from New York Pizza," Ricky quips, referring to the pizza restaurant in Novosibirsk where we went every night seeking familiarity.

I doubt there are places like this in Siberia. In fact, Ricky and I haven't been to a hip restaurant anywhere recently because we've been living on an austere budget. This meal—in fact, this entire diversion to Moscow—is a treat that makes me feel uneasy, but Ricky has helped persuade me that the expense will not break us.

One year ago, Ricky lost his job. He had been working for his brother Jeffrey at a Brooklyn company his father started in the 1960s that sells nuts and bolts. Ricky took the job, one he viewed as beneath him, because he desperately needed to escape financial ruin and an ex-wife in Florida. When he arrived in 1998, he probably thought working for his brother would be a temporary respite from practicing law or at least a reprieve until he figured out what to do next. But when we got together in 2000, he was still there, bored, underutilized, and restless. He made decent money, and although he dreamed of one thing or another, he took no concrete steps to extricate himself. Jeffrey helped him along when he fired him in January 2002. We were shocked—but not really. Jeffrey offered to give him back his job at half the salary. Ricky and I agreed he'd refuse that offer and face the unknown. I knew I could continue to cover our meager expenses with my freelance writing work, and his unemployment checks would help. But we were still undergoing fertility treatments, and I couldn't help but wonder if I was unable to conceive because in my heart I didn't feel like we could support a child. We were thirty-nine years old: ticktock, ticktock.

Since August, Ricky has been building a tea business. He sells loose-leaf teas and herbals and tea-related accessories such as clay and iron pots on the Internet, and he goes to flea markets and corporate venues, too. He's been working hard and the business shows promise, but it doesn't feed us. I've been toiling harder than ever, though writing assignments have dried up since 9/11. It is not a time in our life or in the world at large that feels bountiful and open. It's hard to relax and trust that all will be well, though that's what Ricky says constantly.

I eye the menu and wince. Ricky sees me.

"Stop worrying," he says. "We will never go without. Just order what you want."

At night, I have trouble sleeping. My body is so fatigued, but my mind won't let it rest. *Am I crazy?* I think to myself in the dark. *Should we really bring home a baby before we sort out our financial problems?* We know the adoption agency is not really aware of our circumstances because the application process asked mostly about an earnings history, not current income.

How does Ricky lie there, so sure that everything will be all right, that it will all work out? I have a solid track record of working, but still, what if something happens to me? I don't want to ruin our time in Moscow, so I flick the thoughts away as though they were pesky picnic flies. Finally at 5 AM, still sleepless, I peel myself from under the covers and go to the hotel swimming pool.

Swimming is my refuge from pain, physical or mental. I have learned that by going back and forth, thirty or fifty or seventy times, depending on the length of the pool, I can release whatever shackles me. I have noticed this works even in dire times, like when I got divorced in my early thirties or after my dog died. I don't know if it is the repetitive motion or the muting of sound or the focus on breathing, but something about swimming rescues me temporarily from anxiety. The pool in the Marriott is cool and divine. I am alone. I knife through the water with purpose. I wonder if lack of sleep will make it hard to swim, but surprisingly it doesn't. I keep going for thirty minutes. I find the energy, the purpose, the way one does when one must. Afterward, I lie down on a lounge chair. I try to drift into sleep, but I'm still unable to let go.

I return to the room where Ricky wakes slowly. "Come back to bed," he says.

"No, I'm going to shower. Let's get some breakfast." This excites him, because the Marriott has a spread of smoked fish, herring, fruits, and egg dishes that makes him feel regal. He tosses the covers aside and joins me in the shower.

After breakfast we head to the Metro. The escalator descends so deeply I feel like we're entering a mine. My guidebook tells me that the deepest section of the Metro is 276 feet. I still have remnants of the head cold I had in Novosibirsk, and the deeper we go, the faster my sinuses drain. I'm blowing my nose furiously, but I'm distracted by scores of tattered, lobster-faced souls scattered everywhere in the Metro. Some are slumped over; others are begging with open palms and blank eyes. One woman is spitting and screaming. These are the people who have been lost in the collapse of communism or ensnared in Russia's disease, vodka. Olga's words float back up at me, as do the sorry characters we'd seen lying along the snowy roadside in Novosibirsk.

We leave the Metro to go to the Pushkin State Museum of Fine Arts. Afterward, we walk hand in hand around the Arbat, a cobblestone pedestrian street that is one of the oldest areas in Moscow. It dates back to the fifteenth century, when it was home to artisans, and where Russian nobility lived in the eighteenth century. Now it is lined with overpriced but alluring shops. Street vendors sell everything from Russian soldiers' winter hats to fake KGB IDs to nesting dolls. This winter streetscape has a carnival atmosphere. I notice a lovely china shop. It is filled with the ornate designs Russians favor.

"Let's go in," I say. "Look at this, Ricky." I lift a blue and white teacup with gold accents and gently bring it to my mouth, pinky outstretched. "Isn't this wonderful? Decadent. And look, look at the teapot that goes with it. How lovely! And the sugar bowl," shaped like an elephant. "Aren't elephants good luck?" I am not superstitious—at least I don't think I am.

I'm delighted by the Gzhel, Russian porcelain popularized in the 1830s. It is fancier that anything we own, but there's something about being an adoptive parent that makes you feel as though you should bring back little pieces of your daughter's heritage to her new home. My mind flits between a scene in which I'm serving tea from these beautiful objects and the running tab of what we've been spending. Again, Ricky encourages me, and the saleswoman wraps up four cups, a teapot, and the elephant sugar bowl.

On our last day in Moscow, we go to the GUM (pronounced *goom*) department store, which is a famous glass-encrusted Victorian pile filled with expensive shops. It resembles the grand pavilion at the New York Botanical Garden in the Bronx. A refuge from the near-zero cold, we walk up and down the nearly deserted mall. Like everywhere else in Russia, there are shops filled with fur hats. I go into one and try some on. When I catch a glimpse of myself in the mirror, I feel ashamed.

"That one looks nice on you," Ricky says. "Buy it."

"Don't even . . ."

I grab his hand and we leave the store.

On the way out of the arcades, I notice a children's store. It is fancy. It has the look of the New York City Madison Avenue children's boutique. I peer closer to get a look at a beautiful ivory-white quilted down jacket ringed with a fur hood.

"That jacket is made for Russian winter," I say. "It's precious."

"Let's go in and have a look," Ricky replies.

"Nah, I don't think so. Let's leave it."

I walk away with a pit in my stomach. I want this baby. I want to clothe and protect her, but I'm not ready. She's not real yet. She's in Siberia. I need more time.

Four

I'm thumbing through the newest nonfiction books at Barnes & Noble. The store on Broadway is crowded for mid-morning. I glance around at the mothers pushing strollers, legions of them passing time, filling the aisles and making them impassable. I feel an uncomfortable tug in my gut. That voice, that annoying voice in my head says, *Shouldn't you be buying parenting books? Or at the very least adoptive parenting books?*

Maybe I should. Maybe I should do a lot of things I don't do, like floss more often or make peace with my mother, but I usually give in to my gut and my gut wants to read books on politics or the growing locavore movement. Because I'm thirty-nine, I'm the latecomer to parenting in my circle of friends and family. I never took much of an interest in other people's children, not even my own relatives, but I have watched, with some horror, what I believe is an obsessive, off-kilter generation of parenting. Too many women I know have turned mothering into their life's work. They've left behind careers. Dreams. Ways they were going to change the world. They are obsessed with stroller brands and sleeping schedules and the "right" schools. They are caught up in molding and shaping their children as though they'd all become sculptors and perfection is paramount. They treat their children as though they are their partners—blurring the line between parent and child, vying to be their child's BFF. They've read a lot of books on empowering their children.

They bask in the light they hope will emanate from their offspring. I've not yet walked in their shoes, but to me it seems imbalanced. And it has caused me some ambivalence about child rearing. On the one hand, it's been hard to watch women I know have one baby, then two, and sometimes a third, while I went through a divorce and had at times believed I would never have my own children. On the other hand, I wonder if I will fall into this parenting trap when and if I do become a mother. Part of the problem is groupthink. This helicopter parenting generation feeds off its peers, who read only the kind of books I'm standing here avoiding. They reinforce each other. They are establishing a new norm.

But in the back of my mind I toy with the notion that even if motherhood doesn't need a manual, maybe adoptive parenting does. During the adoption process, I've skipped around websites that advise and inform adoptive parents. I never spent too much time on any of them because they cause me anxiety. I'm already aware that when you adopt, you begin with a big black hole.

You don't know what your baby has been though. What has she eaten? Has she been loved or handled enough? What, if anything, has she been genetically predisposed to be or to do? In Russian adoptions you can't get information about the physical or mental health of the birth parents. You start with a mystery. You accept that, and you go from there. Sure, I could load up on what ifs and psychological terms, but I'd rather not.

I glance back over at the nonfiction books piled up in a pyramid, pull a couple to buy, and head over to the register.

Two hours later, I'm back at my desk. The phone rings. I cringe when I see the caller ID. *Why is the adoption agency calling?* I wonder. We've only been back four days. *They probably want more money.*

"Hello," I say.

"Hi, Tina," says the adoption counselor. "I know you're probably still recovering from your trip, but I have some interesting news."

"Interesting?" I say. "What kind of interesting news?"

"You guys will be traveling within the next ten days to get your baby," she says. "She's from . . . let's see here . . . ah yes, she's from a Siberian orphanage. Yep, that's right. You've got to make arrangements for your next trip."

I hear the words but can't absorb them. I know what she said, but assume I've misheard her. After a long pause, she says, "Tina? Are you there?"

"What?!" I exclaim. "That's not possible. We just returned a few days ago. I'm not even over my jet lag," I say, hoping for a laugh. "No, seriously, we'd been told by our handlers out there that we wouldn't be called back for three to six months. Are you sure you're not making a mistake?"

"Hang on a minute," she says, leaving me on the phone to listen to on-hold music, Patsy Cline singing "Crazy."

I glance at the folders on my desk and mentally calculate my writing deadlines. I break into a sweat even though the apartment is not too warm. I tell myself to calm down. There must be a mistake.

"Hi, sorry to keep you waiting. No, I've got the right information in front of me. Your daughter is ready to go."

"Okay," I say, resigned but clearly not thrilled and increasingly aware that the counselor must be wondering why I want this delayed.

"It's just that, wow, I'm just taken aback," I say, heaving a big breath. "And I don't have anything ready for the baby. I thought I had so much more time."

"Oh, I understand perfectly," she says. "Don't worry—ten days should give you enough time to make travel plans. I'll send you the details by e-mail. Let me know if you have any questions. Bye."

I'm stunned. This must be what it's like to give birth prematurely. You're walking along in your sixth month—thinking you've got three more months to glow, organize spice racks, and decorate a precious nursery, and then boom, all that time is snatched away.

If there were a *Guinness World Records* entry for speediest foreign adoption, ours would win. From the time we shipped the telephone book–thick dossier to our adoption agency last August to what is now the projected date Julia will be in our arms, it will be just six months. Everyone told us adoption takes one to two years. Olga had said we wouldn't be back in Siberia for three to six months.

"At least it will be spring," I had said. But it won't.

Mental preparation is an important part of this transition. We don't have a crib or a single toy. I feel hysterical. I do what I always do when I feel hysterical. I call Ricky.

"Calm down," he says. "You need a sed-a-give." He loves that old *Young Frankenstein* joke. "When I get home, we'll sketch out a plan, and everything will be all right. I'll come home a little bit early," he adds.

I dial my friend Lynn to tell her we're traveling again in ten days.

"Mazel tov!" she shrieks. "This is so exciting."

"I don't have anything for the baby. Nothing! Not even a diaper."

"Why don't you come down here and get Hil's old crib?" she suggests.

"Really?" I say. "You still have Hillary's crib?"

"Could never part with it, but I'd feel so good about lending it to Julia," she adds.

"Okay," I say, "I'll let you know when we're coming to Pennsylvania."

The days are a succession of acquisitions and preparations. I am working off the longest to-do list I've ever had. Ricky and I go to a Babies"R"Us in New Jersey. I have never been in one of these baby superstores. I imagine we need one of everything. We get one of those enormous carts and start filling it with a baby blanket and a crib bumper and a crib sheet. "Where are the pillowcases?" I say.

"Babies don't use pillows," he says.

"They don't?" I ask. We move on to the diapers, formula, pacifiers, baby wipes, baby shampoo, plastic bottles. In no time, the cart is full. This is not how I pictured feathering my baby's nest. I'm not the type of person who shops in a big-box store—*what was I doing in a place like this?*

"Being practical," Ricky reminds me, unsentimental about the need to stock up on what we needed fast and affordably.

"We have a lot to do," he says.

The day after we bring the crib home from Lynn's, we are standing in the foyer that will become Julia's nursery. It is a windowless space of about seven by nine feet. At least our prewar building's ceilings are high and airy, and we've enclosed the space with pretty glass French doors. There will be enough room for the crib, a bureau of drawers and a changing table. The space is too tight to include a rocking chair. Ricky opens up the folded crib, and I gasp.

"What's the matter?"

"It's dusty and scuffed," I say.

"Okay, we'll wipe it down. Let's just get it built first."

It takes about forty minutes to assemble. When it's ready, Ricky rolls it into a corner.

Tears spring from my eyes.

"What's the matter?" he says. "It's not bad. It's pretty, really."

"It's used," I say, dropping to the floor. "I want something that is new. Something that is my own. I appreciate Lynn lending us this but, I don't know. . . . It's just that nothing is the way I thought it would be."

But I stop short at saying what I'm really thinking, which is *I have a used crib for a baby that is not really mine. A used crib and a used baby.* I don't let these thoughts turn to words. They'd be poisonous the second they left my lips.

Ricky comes to me and holds me.

"C'mon, let's make up the crib."

He rips open the bags with the sheet, comforter, and bumper and begins arranging them.

"See, look how cute this is," he says.

The comforter is a patchwork of yellow squares filled with jungle animals. It is precious, and it cheers me up. It was designed by John Lennon.

"You're right," I say. "I'm just feeling overwhelmed."

The next day I go to a travel agent the adoption agency recommended to get travel documents. It is manned by a flame-haired woman who is buried in stacks of paper in a stifling midtown office. She moves back and forth between Russian and English and makes no attempt at being friendly. She reminds me of Olga and of other women we met in Russia. Harsh, unsentimental, no soft edges. I wonder if Julia's genes will carry these traits.

I meet a man named Robert who will be traveling the same day we are. On our first trip to Russia, Ricky and I were alone; we did not encounter any other adoptive parents. But I'm told the second trip will be different. We will be traveling with two other adoptive families to Siberia, and there will be a large contingent of adoptive parents scheduled to fly to Moscow with us. Robert and his wife, Laura, will be collecting their child from Samara, which is about a ninety-minute flight from Moscow. He's intrigued when I tell him we have to go to Siberia—that in fact we have only just returned from Siberia and that I am not looking forward to another round in the gulag. He laughs, which puts me at ease. Robert tells me he and his wife are thinking about bringing back two children because they have been unable to conceive and they don't want to have to go through this adoption process more than once.

"Wow," I say. "Two children. I'm having enough trouble preparing for one," I say.

He smiles again.

"See you in a few days at Kennedy Airport," he says, when he leaves the office.

It's Saturday, the last Saturday night Ricky and I will be free to live it up without a baby-sitter, but I'm dead tired. So is he. I can't remember when we last "lived it up," though it's nice to know the option's there. It's like living in Manhattan. People always say the city has the best museums and theater, but how often do you really do these things when you are preoccupied with settling down and making a family?

Nevertheless, the thought of life with a baby is scary and, in truth, almost impossible for me to picture.

We go over our checklist. Everything is in order.

"We have to pack the 'gifts,'" I say sarcastically.

We have been told by our agency that we are expected to disseminate "gifts" to nearly everyone who handles us. We are bringing silk scarves, the loose-leaf tea we sell, New York paraphernalia such as T-shirts and snow globes and lots of diapers for the orphanage. I don't mind the diapers because they are for the babies.

ooooo

The Chinese delivery boy raps at the door. I'm watching television half-heartedly. While Ricky hands him money, I shriek, "Oh, my God. Oh, my God!"

Ricky practically drops the food. He assumes I've seen a mouse. Or a ghost.

"What's the matter?"

"I haven't bought any clothes for Julia," I moan. "She doesn't have anything. We can't bring her out of the orphanage buck naked, which is how she'll be handed to us, buck naked."

"Okay, calm down. We'll get her some clothes tomorrow. We're not leaving until Wednesday."

"I don't even know what size she is. I've never even bought baby clothes."

"You're just nervous. Everything will be fine, you'll see. Go to Bloomingdale's first thing tomorrow and buy her a whole bunch of clothes. If the sizes are wrong, we'll exchange them. Don't be so afraid."

ooooo

I think back to that fateful day in the fertility clinic last May. For six months I needed to have my blood monitored every other day while we were trying artificial insemination. Ricky came with me every time, which was good because I'm a complete coward when it comes to medical intervention. The technician had wrapped the rubber tourniquet around my arm and told me to make a fist. She already knew I was one of those problematic patients who needed her husband to hold her hand.

"Come on, darling. Try to relax," she had said, wriggling my arm. "I need to find a vein."

Bruised from too many blood tests (or bloodlettings, as I called them), it took three attempts for the nurse to jam in the needle. I felt a searing pain. I started to cry. Ricky rubbed my shoulders. Afterward, I said, "I can't do this anymore."

"Okay, you don't have to," Ricky said, and without skipping a beat he added, "We can adopt. There are millions of babies who need homes."

"Really?" I said, snuffling. Lately, I had been thinking that if I couldn't even tolerate blood tests, how in the world was I going to be able to move on to more aggressive in vitro fertilization treatment with its daily injections? I'm terrified of being put under with anesthetics. How was I going to be able to undergo a surgical egg retrieval of maybe a dozen eggs and then an implantation of multiple embryos? What if I had twins or triplets? In the back of my mind, I knew I wouldn't. I couldn't. I never said anything.

"Ricky, we've never talked about adoption before," I said.

"I know," he said. "But this is grueling for you, and if we move on to in vitro, there's a huge risk of failure, whereas adoption is a sure thing. And, we only have enough money for one attempt. Our COBRA won't even cover the procedure."

I rolled down my sleeve, stood up, and hugged this man who seemed too good to be true. I might not be able to make a baby with him, but I knew then and there that no matter what, we'd always be able to muddle through our darkest hours. I felt like the luckiest woman in that fertility clinic that day—the one who walked out, never to return.

I arrive at Bloomingdale's on 59th and Lexington, breathless. The door is locked. I cup my hands around my cold face and peer through the steamy, tinted glass. It's five to ten, and my teeth are chattering. Standing alone on the frosty street, my mind drifts back to a time when shopping here with my mother was the most natural thing in the world. Shopping was love; shopping was sustenance; shopping was what we did. Especially before the start of each and every season. If she were here with me now and I was twelve again, we'd be shopping for bathing suits and lacy coveralls for a winter break in Puerto Rico. This might be the one place where she wouldn't constantly flick her wrist to see what time it was. We'd have grabbed ten bathing suits, definitely bikinis, before slipping into the dressing room. She'd let out a sigh of relief while settling into a chair, letting her heavy pocketbook fall to the floor. She was a beautiful woman, still. She'd been a bleached blonde practically my whole life. She had large blue eyes and good bone structure, but she had a complicated life with my father, and the strain of their relationship tightened her face. I was the most important person in her world, which must have made me feel useful. I'd model the bikinis, one at a time.

"What do you think of this one?" I'd ask, seeking her approval.

"That suits your figure," she'd say, looking up and down, pleased at the sight of my slender body. "See if they have that one in another color or pattern. You could always use an extra suit."

After she'd paid for the suits, she'd hand me the big brown bag and say, "Use everything in good health." Then, she'd pause. "But don't tell your father what we bought today."

It was an odd thing to say, because there never was any detectable shortage of money. But I never asked why she said that. It made our shopping ventures seem like a clandestine mission between mother and daughter. I realized years later that she was subconsciously trying to alienate me from my father by creating secrets between us he couldn't be privy to—secrets that didn't even matter but secrets just the same.

∞∞∞

I'm startled when I hear the sound of keys jiggling the front door. An effete man dressed in an impeccable wool suit leans his head outside and says, "Welcome to Bloomingdale's." He doesn't know I've been here a million times. I look as though it's my first visit.

"Can I help you?" he sing-songs, tilting his head one way and then the other.

"Do you, are the, do, where are babies' clothes?" I stammer.

"They're on the lower level," he says, sweeping his arm in a balletic gesture toward an escalator. "Right down there," he points for emphasis.

I hear my heart thumping in my chest. I am in a foreign world when I reach the bottom of the escalator. Teeny clothes hang on wee hangers, and neat piles of shirts and pants are stacked on tables. They look like dolls' clothes. I should be delighted, but I'm dizzy and disoriented. I'm buying baby clothes for my baby who's not here, whom I don't even know. It's another reminder of how upside down mothering can be when you're adopting a baby and you're shopping for her and you can only hazily picture her height and girth. I must look like I've stumbled into a postnuclear world. An African American saleswoman comes over and gently says, "May I help you?"

"Um, yes, I need baby clothes, for a baby, my baby, but she's not here now."

She looks at me quizzically for a moment. "I think I understand. Come with me."

As I trail her I keep stammering. "Yes, I'm adopting a baby. She's seven months, and I'm going to get her in Siberia in a few days."

"Siii-beeeeeer-iii-aa?" she says while clearing her throat. "Well, well, darling, I think we better look at some of these old winter clothes we have right here. Some are even on sale. C'mon, honey." I trot behind her like a duckling following its mother. She hands me tiny snowsuits, and I hold them up and eyeball them.

"I like the yellow one," I say. It is a one-piece suit with a hood. It's fuzzy, and it has pink swirly buttons. I hold it up to my cheek and try to imagine what it will be like to see Julia's little face poking through the hood. "Yes, this is good."

Yellow seems like a good color for starting a new life. Like the sun coming up. A new day. A new life. Better than pink. I remember that her crib quilt is also yellow.

∞∞∞

For the next forty-five minutes, I look at nearly every piece of clothing for a one-year-old baby. This kindly woman is the mother who is not here for me now. I wish my mother was here with me now, but our relationship has been strained for a decade. There's no intimacy or shared moments, only anger—anger because so many things have gone wrong and they can't be put right. Everyone says things will change when I bring Julia home, that giving her a granddaughter will give us another chance.

Our rift started when I got divorced in 1994. I had married an Englishman who seemed to her like Prince Charming. My marriage was filled with jet-set travel and diamonds. I waited for real life to begin, but it never did. My mother could not understand how I could walk away from such financial security.

Even through the process of adoption, tensions between my mother and I have not melted.

By the time I'm ready to leave, I have filled two big brown bags.

"You're gonna have the best-dressed baby around," she says while ringing up the clothes. "And the warmest."

I suppress tears. I'm afraid if I cry she'll be compelled to put her arms around me until I stop. I get a hold of myself. "I can't tell you how much your help has meant to me. Thank you."

"That's no problem," she says. "Now you enjoy that baby of yours, sweetheart."

I leave the store and hail a cab. Julia has a wardrobe. A brand-new, unused wardrobe with tags on clothing that is crisp and neat and unstained. I recall how the orphanage had her dressed in threadbare, mismatched clothes.

Yes, yellow is optimistic.

Five

"Hey, there's Robert," I say to Ricky. "The guy I told you about. The one I met at the Russian travel office."

He is with a tall, statuesque woman with a thick mane and heavily painted face that conceals her age. That must be Laura. They are mingling with a group of couples. We will all be on the Delta flight to Moscow within a couple of hours. Our lives changed forever.

Some are carrying strollers.

"Ricky, look. They're carrying strollers. We don't have a stroller."

Ricky cranes his head over the newspaper he's reading.

"Hmm, I don't think we'll need a stroller. We'll be with Julia for three days in Moscow. We'll use the Snugli."

I sink back into my chair.

Julia is only seven months old. A Snugli should work. Robert had told me the baby (or babies) they'd be adopting were thirteen months old. It is still a mystery how we were able to get such a young infant. We'd been told from the start that most babies adopted from Russian orphanages were, at minimum, a year old. Of course we wrote in our application we wanted the youngest female baby possible, but still, it seemed like an anomaly to be getting such a young child. Was there something to be suspicious about, or were we incredibly lucky?

Robert bounces over to us. He is a wiry, balding man with deep chocolate eyes and a come-hither smile.

"Hi," I say. "Robert, right?"

"Yes, that's right, good memory. This is Laura," he says.

Laura smiles weakly. She lets Robert do the socializing.

"This is Ricky," I say.

"So, are you guys ready?" he asks.

"Ready as one can be," I say.

"Yeah, this is nerve-racking," he concedes.

"Where are your seats?" he asks.

The plane begins to board.

"See you on the plane," he says, waving his airline ticket as he walks away.

While waiting for the plane to lift off, I wonder what kinds of anguish these prospective parents have gone through to get to this place. We are sitting on what is dubbed Delta's "Orphan Express." I look around at the faces. These women are the women we all know. They're thin and fat and attractive and plain and thirty-five and forty-two. All of them, I'd bet, have taken a swipe at fertility treatments. Robert had told me that Laura had undergone five rounds of in vitro fertilization, and although they conceived twice, they lost the baby each time. By the time you're traveling on the Orphan Express, you don't imagine much else can go wrong because you've meticulously filled out paperwork, you've been vetted, and you've shelled out a fortune, sometimes your life savings, to make this happen. If you're like me, you're thinking: *I just have to get through this trip and, well, somehow we'll make it work.*

Throughout the adoption process, I'd felt alone, except for Ricky's support. When we first received the grainy videotape of Julia, we shared it with friends and family at Thanksgiving dinner, and everyone cooed and cheered. But in the months that followed, the process of readying myself to become a parent was solitary and lonely. No one suggested a baby shower. No one asked how I was feeling. No one told me I was glowing. Our tales from the first trip to Siberia amused friends and family as a travelogue or a magazine article, but I wasn't embraced by a tribe of female relations who would have treated me like a newly enrolled member if I had been pregnant. I wasn't surrounded by mama bears wanting to dole out advice. I didn't get the key to the club, like my younger sister did, each time she'd announced she was pregnant.

ꝏꝏꝏ

Shortly before the end of the ten-hour flight, Robert walks down the aisle and stops. Breakfast has just been served.

He leans in and asks, "How are you guys doing?"

"Long flight," I say. "How are you guys doing?"

"Laura slept most of the way. I got a little shut-eye."

"I can't sleep on planes," I say.

"Well, maybe we'll need to get used to not sleeping," he says, chuckling, but I can see the fear in his eyes about the change that will soon occur. Robert is nearly fifty. He's had a long time to become accustomed to living without children.

As the plane makes its final descent, a group of Russian men sitting in front of us stand up and open the overhead storage bins to get their carry-ons. The flight attendant implores them to sit down, but they won't listen. They are not terrorists—just arrogant and lawless.

"Typical Russians," my husband says.

"They're crazy," I say.

"It's a reaction to living under communist rule for too long," Ricky says. "They're throwing off the chains of oppression."

This makes me wonder again about Julia and her genes. What are her birth parents like? Will she be genetically inclined to break rules, to flout authority? I'd never given too much thought to the nature/nurture argument. Would she necessarily be like me or Ricky if she carried our DNA? Come to think of it, we were both a bit antiestablishment. Maybe Julia's deck is stacked. A future rebel.

We are driven in a van to the Moscow Marriott and will be leaving for Siberia later this evening. Some of the adoptive parents who are traveling to closer cities will spend the night in Moscow. When we get to the hotel, there is a mixup. They don't have a room for us to use for a few hours. I'm about to cry because I know how hard the journey gets from here—a harrowing six-hour flight to Siberia on a Soviet-era plane that makes the insides of your stomach fall like jet-fuel flotsam. I was counting on a respite before the next leg. "Moscow Olga" is trying to arrange something with the clerk at the desk, but it seems hopeless. The hotel is booked. Then a woman from our group steps forward.

"Why don't you guys take our room for a few hours?" she says. "We're not leaving until the morning."

Before Ricky could say something like, "We can't possibly," I squeal, "Oh, my God, thank you, thank you so much! That is so nice of you—are you sure?"

"Sure, here, take the key. You can leave it at the front desk. My husband and I are going to go out and sightsee for a few hours."

Moments like this make you wonder if angels are put in your path to help you believe you're on the right road. Ricky doesn't believe in angels. He believes in the kindness of strangers.

We ride the elevator to our borrowed room. I shower. Ricky lies on the bed.

When I come out he says, "Let's order some porn. They'll be pretty shocked when they get the bill."

I crack up because I know he's kidding. To the outside world, Ricky appears so straight, but I know better. Life has blessed him with a very dark sense of humor.

The flight to Novosibirsk is much like the first one. It's snowing. The plane is creaky and old. The bathrooms are unusable, the food inedible. Knowing what to expect helps a bit. At least I'm not sick as a dog this time. But again I'm not sure I won't end up a statistic of Russian aviation.

My mind drifts. I can't sleep. I'm eighteen, learning I'm pregnant after a summer at sleepaway camp. I was in love for the first time. My hippie boyfriend David and I had sex a few times. Once in a motel, where we stayed the night, another time on a grassy knoll overlooking the lake. I had come home at the end of August, and I was in my mother's bedroom looking in the mirror. I just knew, somehow, that I had a baby growing inside me. I wasn't hysterical at first, but when the tests confirmed my hunch, there was never a choice or a discussion. It was assumed this was a problem that had to be fixed, and my mother, who had always been my confidante, took care of all the details. David was a loving and sympathetic voice in the days leading up to "the procedure."

It was a late summer day. Hot and humid. My mother drove to the Manhattan clinic. She suggested I think of the procedure as a tooth extraction. I tried. I was stripped naked, my legs in stirrups. They injected my hand, and the pain seared through my arm. I woke nauseated and groggy. I cried, but I wasn't sure why. I took painkillers for the cramps. David visited me the next day. My father could not look at him or at me. It never occurred to me I'd gotten rid of a baby I might have wanted. "Move forward" was always my mother's advice. I was on my way to my sophomore year at college. Having an abortion is nothing like a tooth extraction. Having an abortion leaves a void you may or may not know about. It could take years, like when you're near forty and unable to conceive, when the weight of the experience revisits, making you remember it as though it was recent. It can take twenty years to cry for that lost child. Infertility made me mourn the child I might have had and the one I will never have. I wonder what is worse, mourning an aborted baby or giving one life and then abandoning it to someone "more suitable."

∞∞∞

I recognize Vladimir's expressionless face right away this time. It is morning, but we are in Siberia's postdawn darkness, back at the cavernous airport, driving again in his Volga. Déjà vu.

This time around we are not going to the Centralnaya Hotel. When we had returned from the first trip, I'd called our adoption agency and told them I wanted to stay in Novosibirsk's business hotel, which was down the street from the Centralnaya Hotel. I thought there might at least be toilet seats and hot water. Like so many conundrums in Russia, we weren't allowed to switch to the better hotel during the first trip. Ricky's guess was that every step of our trip was rigged to benefit someone who had a hand in the cookie jar. Nothing was flexible. Payoffs at every stop. But a loud enough fuss made back on US soil has landed us in an apartment building. We will be staying there with two other adoptive families: Barbara and Neal, who are adopting a boy, and Jo, a single parent who's here for a girl. The five of us will be living in three apartments and traveling as a group.

"Oh, great," I say to Ricky, as Vladimir's car slows down in the courtyard of a Soviet-style block of multistory concrete buildings. "This time we're staying in a tenement."

"Shhh," Ricky says. "Stay positive. Like you promised."

We lug our stuff up to the second floor. We hear a blood-curdling scream from behind an apartment door. Everyone is too stunned to say anything.

Our flat is a two-bedroom apartment with a large living room, a tiny kitchen, and a bathroom. I notice the toilet doesn't have a seat. The carpets and textiles are worn and drab, but the apartment is spick-and-span clean. It smells like ammonia. It reminds me of the orphanage. At least we have a refrigerator and a stove. There is a television with one station and a large clock on the wall.

I pull up the shade in the living room window to let light in.

Does Julia's mother live in a grim apartment block like this with her husband and the first two children she gave birth to? Does she stay at home with the babies? Does she know people from the other side of the world are going to take her Yulia away and become her parents?

Russian adoptions are closed. We will never know Maria G. I wonder if the name on our documents is even real. I wonder whether her birth mother feels our presence. Will she mourn Yulia on the anniversaries of her birth?

Barbara is pale and middling. She comes alive when she talks about Amelia, her little girl who is back home with her grandparents. She likes to show pictures of the girl, who is blonde with big blue eyes. She looks nothing like Barbara or Neal, who is thin with dark hair and dark eyes. The couple adopted this child three years ago from Russia. Barbara loves this child. Amelia sustains her. The couple decided to adopt a second child, this time a boy. Neal traveled alone to Russia on the first trip to meet Boris in Orphanage Number Two. He's nearly ten months old. Barbara stayed at home with their daughter, but both of them have to be here for the final adoption in a Russian court. Barbara is uneasy. Her eyes shift back and forth nervously. She sweats a lot, which is not easy to do in Siberia. Only talking about her daughter eases her. She tells us the first adoption went smoothly, and her daughter is a dream. We are sharing stories in a ground-floor room in our apartment block that seems to have been set up for traveling Americans. Women in babushkas are serving us toast and overcooked hard-boiled eggs. We are refueling before Olga and Vladimir come to take us to Orphanage Number Two.

Jo, who lives in Washington, DC, is here to adopt a girl. She has an adopted daughter back in the states who is originally from India. Jo's Russian child, who's almost two years old, is at a different orphanage, so she will be taken in a separate car.

In the company of these women, I am the little sister. Ironically, I feel like the pregnant woman being thrown a baby shower. They're only too happy to dole out mothering advice. This is as close as I've gotten to a communal experience around motherhood.

∞∞∞

We are traveling through stark, monotone streets to Orphanage Number Two, which is less than five minutes away. No one is chatting. Will Julia remember us? I imagine it must be unnerving for babies to be handed off to a pair of strangers who make entirely different verbal sounds from the ones they are used to.

Boris is a fleshy baby with a large head. Barbara and her husband will rename him Brandon. He is clutching his caretaker ferociously, wailing, when Barbara tries to hold him. Barbara makes cooing sounds, but the baby screams louder and louder. She is growing increasingly agitated.

Eventually the baby is soothed enough to be placed in Barbara's open arms. This is the first time she is meeting her baby.

"Here's Julia," Ricky says.

I spin around and see her in another caretaker's arms, smiling just the way she was the first time I met her. She reminds me of a tiny beauty queen flirtatiously winking at admirers. She doesn't make a fuss when she is placed in my arms.

"Maybe she remembers us?" I say to Ricky.

"Hello, baby Julia," I say in a hushed voice. "Do you remember us? We are going to be your parents. I hope you're okay with that. I have bought you the most beautiful yellow snowsuit."

She doesn't cry or resist being held. She also doesn't cling or clutch.

"Do you want to hold her?"

Ricky bends down and lifts her off my lap. He does everything with ease. There's no continuous reel of dialogue looping through his head. Things just arc what they are. I envy his cohesiveness.

We are led, along with Barbara and Neal, to the large gymnasium.

We sit on the mat with Julia, who cannot sit up by herself. "Don't worry, that's normal," Olga tells us. Boris's new parents are fifteen feet away. The room is enormous and spare. Ricky is supporting Julia's back to keep her in a seated position. I'm trying to tempt her with a ball. Once again she seems most intrigued by the large window filtering in light. When we let her relax backward, we notice she is strangely contorting her body, arching her back over and over.

"What is she doing?" I ask Ricky, feeling panicky.

"I'm not sure," he says. I notice he looks uneasy, which is unusual.

We watch her do this again and again.

"Pick her up," I say to Ricky.

I get up and look for Olga. I ask her to come and watch what the baby is doing.

Olga comes to the gym, a little peeved. She stands over the baby, her lips pursed. Ricky lets Julia back down on the mat, and she arches her back again.

"Oh, this," Olga says. "This is nothing. Sometimes children in orphanages have this kind of trouble. They're stretching because their muscles are tight because they don't get enough activity. They spend too much time in the crib, you know. It's perfectly normal."

Ricky and I look at each other. Olga is our only conduit to explanations. We have to take it or leave it.

Over my left shoulder, I hear a fuss. Barbara and Neal seem to be arguing over something. We shift our attention over there. Barbara is squatting behind a bench, poking up and down like a meerkat, playing peekaboo. The baby is unresponsive. Barbara beckons Olga.

"This baby doesn't seem to be responding," she says. "He won't make eye contact. He won't play peek-a-boo."

"We do not play peek-a-boo," Olga says in a stern response.

Barbara looks like she's about to collapse.

I don't know whether to laugh or cry. We are in *The Twilight Zone*. Everything is surreal.

Just then, a bevy of little girls drifts into the gymnasium. Some are wearing dresses. They are blonde, and they range in age from three to five. They look like a nursery school class. They dance around in a circle. They have large foreheads, thin lips, and eyes set wide apart. They suffer from fetal alcohol syndrome and other ailments because their mothers drank through pregnancy. This is what Olga explained when I asked what will happen to these children. From the look in her eyes, I know these are the "damaged" children—the ones who never end up in grainy videos sent to adoptive parents.

I remember what the pediatrician had said when she saw Julia's tape and medical records. She was one of those pediatricians who specializes in evaluating the health of foreign adoptees based on records and videos. They are a cottage industry in America. There's a whole crop of these doctors, and they know adoptive parents hang on their every word because the Russian medical records are indecipherable, even though they are translated in English.

"This is as good as it gets," she had said over the phone.

"What does that mean?" I'd asked.

"From what I can tell, she looks healthy, and the good thing is she's very young so you'll have a chance to reverse any of the negative consequences of her early months."

Are we to believe we can reverse these early damages? *Yes, yes,* we tell ourselves. *Yes, absolutely, we have enough love to compensate for what they've lost.* We will undo the damage, wipe their slates clean, as though they are Etch A Sketch pads. We will love and adore them and make them feel as though they were born the moment we took them away from the ammonia and tiny cots where they are virtually imprisoned with swaddling blankets and left to suck on cold-tea concoctions. We will replace these first memories with the aroma of fresh-baked apple pie and a crib with a spinning animal mobile.

∞∞∞

After we've returned the babies to the caretakers, Barbara is crying hysterically. Neal is trying to soothe her. Olga is attempting to hush-hush her. Disruptions in the orphanage are frowned upon.

I ask Olga what's wrong.

She curtly says Barbara is upset and walks away.

We hear Neal say to her, "Take your time. If you don't want to bring him home, we won't."

A shock rips through my body.

Barbara is considering leaving the baby behind. How could she? How cruel that seems. What would I do if I felt that way? I'm glad I don't. Those back-arching movements have scared me but not enough for me to reconsider my decision. Maybe Barbara's unstable. I don't know what to think.

We are ushered from the room and taken back to our apartment block. Barbara and Neal hurry up the steps and close their door.

"Wow, that's got to be torture," I say to Ricky.

"Yeah, she seems a bit kooky."

"You know what I think?" I say, not waiting for him to answer. "I think that Barbara is very happy with her family of three, and somewhere along the way she convinced herself she needs a brother for her daughter, and here she is, ten thousand miles away from her daughter, and she's miserable and wants to go home and has no interest in this child."

"Could be," Ricky says. "I just think she's a bit wacky."

A couple of hours later, Vladimir returns to take us into the business district for lunch and free time. Only Neal comes downstairs.

"Where's Barbara?" I ask.

"She's lying down," he says. "She's not feeling too well."

I'm not sure what to say. I don't know what I can say that would be at all helpful.

Happily, he's willing to talk. "She's concerned about the baby," he says. "She's afraid he's not going to be able to bond with her."

"Can she really know that from meeting him just one time?" I ask.

"Well, with our daughter, she fell in love instantly," he says. "She just felt like her mother immediately, but this time it feels different."

"Maybe it's because he's a boy?" I say, thinking but not saying I have not fallen in love with Julia either as of yet. She is beautiful and I'm not having second thoughts about taking her home, but my heart has not given way to some convulsive feeling of passion.

"Maybe," Neal says, pausing.

"Barbara's done a lot of reading about Reactive Attachment Disorder," he continues.

"What's that?" Ricky says.

"It's a syndrome that is not that uncommon among kids who've spent their early months or years institutionalized in orphanages. By the time they are adopted, they often have trouble bonding or attaching."

"Oh, I'm sure that's the exception and not the rule," I say. "It seems your first Russian adoption has been successful."

"Yeah, Barbara bonded with our daughter Amelia right away."

"I think everything will turn out fine with Brandon," I say.

"Yes. I'm sure that most times things turn out fine. But there are many documented cases of Reactive Attachment Disorder, especially from Romanian orphanages, and from Russian ones, too. Sometimes it's okay. But sometimes these kids are not all right. They can be very difficult to live with. They have a lot of emotional problems, and it can be really disruptive for the whole family."

I look at Ricky. He is listening intently. I think back to the day in the bookstore when, perhaps, I should have picked up a book or two on foreign adoption.

Neal sees he's unnerved me.

"Well, don't worry. Your baby seems very animated. I'm sure it will all work out as it's supposed to." I accept his answer, believing Brandon and Julia are so fundamentally different that I don't need to worry about the scary words he's just uttered.

Six

We are dropped off at a cafeteria-style café. We line up and put our food on trays. We invite Neal to sit with us, and he does. He discusses his work. I chat about my writing career, telling him I worked at New Jersey newspapers for ten years. Barbara is a teacher, but she's taken time off to raise their child. Ricky talks a little about the tea company.

During lunch, I notice a group of young women, maybe twenty-year-olds. They peel off heavy fur coats. Underneath they are wearing thin leggings with pencil skirts and baby-doll shirts. There are three of them, and they're all tall and gorgeous with long, golden hair, exquisite paper-white complexions, and broad cheeks with slightly slanted eyes.

Is this Julia in twenty years? I can picture her dark, slightly slanted eyes and her alabaster skin.

Siberia is a crossroads of European and Asian cultures. Its very name conjures up images of prison camps and frozen death. Siberia equals banishment. It's the place people never return from. Or go to, unless they are forced to.

Novosibirsk, with 1.5 million people, is Siberia's largest city. It has its own narrative, according to the few bits of information I had been able to scrounge on the Internet before we left. The city was founded in 1893 at the future site of a Trans-Siberian Railway bridge crossing the great

Siberian river Ob. Since 1925, it has been the center of heavy metallurgy and machine-tool manufacturing, of international trade conferences, and of mining and chemical manufacturing. The Ob River, one of the longest in the world, runs through the broad, wide city, flowing toward the Arctic. The river is so polluted with industrial waste and toxic oil it doesn't entirely freeze in winter. There's a world-class opera and ballet house here. In the 1950s, the Soviet government built Akademgorodok, a scientific research complex located on the city's outskirts. Novosibirsk has fourteen research institutions and universities.

Neal says he's going to walk around and get some fresh air. Ricky gets us each another cup of black tea, and we linger a bit longer. "Wow, I don't envy him," I say. "Barbara probably blames him for coming here alone and not seeing that the baby is a problem."

"I don't know," he says, blowing on the steamy cup. "She seems a bit neurotic. I feel sorry for him."

"What would you do if I suddenly had a change of mind?"

"C'mon," he says. "Let's go see what we can find to like about Novosibirsk."

It is cold, but the frigid air is rejuvenating. Our first stop is a store that sells maps. None of the maps are in English. We've been wanting desperately to have a map, because we constantly feel disoriented. We're driven everywhere by Vladimir. We're never allowed to take public transportation. Ricky says they drive us a different route from our housing digs to the orphanage every time just to keep us off our game.

We duck into an Internet café. It is up one level and filled with grungy twenty-somethings. They scowl when they see us. The computer is slow. Our friend Jay has been staying at our apartment with our cat. He's our only lifeline. His e-mails are peppered with adorable things Floopy has done. He reports on the cat's eating and bathroom habits. He mentions how tense things are as President George W. Bush prepares to start a war in Iraq.

I sign off with a heavy heart. What grief will a war in Iraq bring? Will New York be targeted again by terrorists? I have not been the same since 9/11. The horrific attack left me unable to feel unfettered and free in a city I've loved my whole life. I wasn't at Ground Zero. I only knew people who knew people who died. But I was changed. I stopped riding the subway, I became claustrophobic in high-rises, and I didn't like to be in places with crowds. I craved a little cabin in the woods we could escape to at the drop of a hat. As I reread Jay's words about Bush waging war, I think maybe we should stay here in this frozen city at the end of the world.

"You OK?" Ricky asks.

"The neocons are marching to war," I say.

"Yeah, I saw that too. Onward Christian soldiers."

"What if we stayed here?" I say. "What if we stay in the lost corner of the world where presumably nothing awful ever happens? I bet the people here have never even heard about 9/11."

"I don't know about that," he says. "We might be in a remote place but, look, you're on the Internet. I don't think these people are some aboriginal tribe cut off from the world."

Of course he is right. It's been about a decade since Novosibirsk has been opened to the West. There are glimmering signs of capitalism all around us. Still, this place feels like the end of the world to me. A safe house, ironically.

The next day we go to court to finalize the adoption. I had brought a skirt to wear, thinking it'd be important to look nice, but I cannot bear to wear hose and expose my legs to this frost. On the ride to court, we are coached; we are told what will be asked and what we should say. This all seems ridiculous, like all the bureaucracy we've been exposed to before, but, like good monkeys, we respond on cue. Even though this is a formality—and we're told the courts never deny an adoption—my stomach is filled with butterflies. "What if . . ." We've come this far. "Can you imagine?" I say to Ricky.

"It'll be fine."

I've learned there's only one thing that rattles Ricky, and that's a day on the slopes, skiing. When he was twelve he was skiing in the Catskills with his two older brothers. They abandoned him on an icy day, and he broke his leg. He was laid up in bed for months and needed to be home tutored for the rest of seventh grade. He never skied again. When we fell in love in 2000, he knew how much I loved to ski, and he dusted himself off and clipped on a set of skis. It's only when we drive up to the mountains that he grows quiet and pensive. I guess he needs to be afraid of something. Today, he's not worried. It's not that his training as a lawyer makes this process more decipherable; he simply trusts things will turn out okay. He often says, "I know the sun will rise every morning."

The court session is quick and painless. We are asked a couple of questions by a panel of administrators. Olga translates. "Congratulations," she says when we leave the tiny courtroom. The next stop is the ticketing office to buy airline tickets from Siberia back to Moscow. Olga had explained we couldn't do this in advance because there was uncertainty as to how many days we would have to spend in Novosibirsk.

∞∞∞

On our last day in the city, we are free until 9:00 PM, when we will be taken to the orphanage to collect Julia. Vladimir drives us to a local crafts market, which is a warren of art and collectibles. I buy some old maps of Novosibirsk.

"One day I'll want to write about this godforsaken place," I tell Ricky. "It will be good to have a map."

"Hopefully by then you'll have mastered Russian," he says.

I thumb through the artwork. The place is dank and musty, but I come across a few pieces I like. We buy a six-by-six-inch framed enamel of a mélange of Russian-style buildings overlapping each other. "Novosibirsk" is written on the painting in English. It is signed by "Shylaga."

"Very good artist. Local artist," says the purveyor, a bulky man with a thick black mustache.

Ricky leans in and says, "They're probably made in a factory in China."

Perhaps, but we like it.

Then I notice a pair of whimsical painted kittens with oversized eyes and curious expressions. "These really are sweet. I am going to buy these and hang them in Julia's room."

On the way to the orphanage that night, we are told to be very fast. Julia will be handed to us naked. "Don't talk to anyone. Dress her quickly. Be very quiet."

"How *noir*," I say to Ricky.

"Shh," he says. "We have our instructions."

Olga tiptoes up the steps. We follow her lead. Everything is done with Japanese-knife-tossing speed. Ricky pulls on a diaper, then a onesie, and then the yellow snowsuit, but there's no time to admire it. After she is dressed, Ricky sweeps her into his arms. There is a pacifier in her mouth. It has a plastic yellow and white daisy around it. I'm handed a tiny little cardboard box. I take a moment to lift the lid. Inside is a little gold baptismal cross. I fight back tears as I think of Julia's young birth mother, who will never again see her child.

Driving to the airport, I notice Julia is fascinated with the moonlight, just as she was with sunlight. What a phenomenon—a world outside the thick walls where she has lived her whole tiny life.

It is starting to snow. Again, we will be flying through a storm.

"How many times can we defeat death?" I say to Ricky.

"Don't worry," he says. "We'll be back at the Moscow Marriott before you know it."

I hook my mind on the marble lobby and the Marriott's serene swimming pool in an attempt to calm down. Olga leads us to the airport lounge, where we sit with Barbara, Neal, and Brandon, and Jo and her child.

Olga is speaking in a hushed voice to the agent at the desk. Then she turns and says, "The flight is going to be delayed due to the storm."

"What?" I say. "We've flown through worse than this. I don't understand."

By now Olga has become accustomed to my neurosis, but she is done with us. We have our baby. She says good-bye hastily and wishes us good luck.

I look at Barbara, who is holding Brandon on her lap. She must have gone through hell to get to this point of acceptance. She actually seems rather peaceful. She's probably counting down the hours until she can get back to New Jersey and her daughter. Jo doles out Cheerios to her little girl, who has thin black hair and a rash all over her face. I think to myself how brave Jo must be, a single mother, bringing home a child who looks like she's never had a day of decent care. But Jo is chipper and upbeat.

Ricky checks in with the desk about departure times, but he's not getting much information. He chats with a German businessman who is in Siberia to sell machine tools. His English is perfect. Julia sits on my lap. I feed her formula from a bottle. She seems to like it. Briefly, I feel like a mother. Then, a loud pop, followed by a putrid stench.

"Oh, my God!" I scream, feeling the hot ooze of diarrhea cover my lap.

Ricky leaps from his seat and grabs her. He knows what to do. He peels off the yellow jumpsuit. Barbara and Jo jump in to help, handing Ricky baby wipes and plastic bags to dispose of the soiled diaper. Barbara digs in her bag for a clean diaper. There is a veritable factory of baby care, but I am frozen solid. I can't change a diaper. How can I be this child's mother? Barbara's looking at me—probably thinking, *Now who's the crazy one?*

"Don't worry," Barbara says wryly. "Motherhood is a learning process."

Throughout the diaper explosion episode, Julia never cries. Come to think of it, I have yet to see her cry. Don't all babies cry?

ထထထ

Two hours later, we are called to board. I'm glad to have Novosibirsk behind me.

The staff at the Moscow Marriott is accustomed to adoptive parents from the United States. They have made a makeshift crib out of a laundry basket for Julia. Julia sleeps through the first night. We wake on February 14, Valentine's Day. When Ricky and I started dating two and a half years ago, he told me he hated Valentine's Day because of his ex-wife. This woman, whom Ricky and I never mention by name, brought him to his knees financially. She spent the money he made as a criminal defense attorney faster than he could make it. On Valentine's Day she expected to be showered with flowers and jewelry. Ricky maintained the charade long after he'd realized he had married a gold digger. We treat Valentine's Day casually, writing love poems and staying home and cooking dinner. Here we are in Moscow, with our new baby, experiencing the living poetry of becoming parents. Ricky is wearing Julia in a sling. When I try her on, so to speak, I am shocked at how heavy she is around my neck. I can't support her because I have a weak back. At fifteen pounds, Julia feels like a solid sack of potatoes or a small bag of cement.

That morning, I run out to the drugstore for formula. It takes an hour to make myself understood, but the clerk is patient. In between a day of bureaucratic stops to fill out papers, we take Julia with us to lunch. Every time Ricky or I give her formula, I suck in my breath and wait for our modern-day Pompeii to rip. The last stop is another government compound where Julia is checked by a doctor. There are so many questions I'd like to ask. I try to explain the back-arching, but I know the doctor doesn't understand me or won't let on that he does. He examines her in five minutes, as though she were a piece of meat being inspected by a USDA official. Would these doctors ever reveal there was a problem if they had found one this far along in the process? I doubt it.

The next morning we have the lavish buffet breakfast the Marriott serves.

"Hey guys, how's it going?"

We haven't seen Robert and Laura since that first night in Moscow, but his melodic voice is familiar even before I see him. He is carrying

Noa, who has a full head of silk-black hair and a caramel complexion. She looks like a tiny gypsy. Robert tells us she's eleven months old, but she looks at least a year older than Julia, who is completely bald.

"Where's Laura?" I ask.

"She's upstairs on the phone to her mother," he snorts. "She's emotionally overcome by this whole thing. She's a little upset because we were planning on adopting two babies, but it didn't work out."

"We'll . . . ," he continued, hoping to keep talking. "We'll see you guys later at the American Embassy."

"I guess this really is a tough thing for a lot of women," I say to Ricky.

He tells me he's going to the buffet to refill his plate.

There are about fifty couples at the American Embassy, the next to last step in the adoption. They are sitting in rows of chairs with their newly adopted babies. I scan the room, across one row of chairs, then the next, and the next. Uncannily, it looks like the babies have been matched to the parents, like a scarf to a suit.

"How do they do that?" I say, in complete bewilderment.

I look at Julia.

No one would say she resembles me or Ricky, but she does have a small, scoop nose like mine and large, broad cheekbones like Ricky's.

"That's incredible," I continue. "Look at the parents and the babies and tell me what you see."

Ricky scans the rows.

"Wow, they look like the parents!" he says.

I'm not crazy.

"I guess that's why they ask for pictures of us when we fill out the dossier," he says.

"This is like a science fiction movie."

Russian children are easier to blend into their American families than their counterparts from China or Ethiopia. But flying now on the "Orphan Express," it's easy to identify newly minted families. A woman is sitting across the aisle from me. She's traveling with a girl, about two years old. The child is inconsolable, rolling around on the floor, braying like a distressed donkey. There is nothing the woman can say or do to break the child's fit. Even the flight attendant, fluent in Russian, is powerless. I look at the woman sympathetically.

"She's been like this for three days," she says. "I'm at my rope's end."

I smile and debate whether to strike up conversation or simply say I understand when the captain comes over the intercom to tell us about the flight details. All around me I'm reminded of how daunting this process is. I can't say that anyone who was handling us during this adoption process gave us any warning. Sometimes these children are just not all right.

PART TWO

Sometimes These Kids Are Not Alright

Seven

How many times have I returned to Kennedy Airport, thrilled to be back on American soil and looking forward to returning to my apartment to download the experience I've just had? It's not like that today. There's a baby in the back seat of our Honda, and it feels like we've returned with a little alien. As long as we keep driving, as long as this experience remains an adventure in motion, it remains just that, an adventure. But we are heading home, and everything that has defined home up to this point will be different. I have a daughter. I am a mother. I thought I might feel relief or elation, but I'm weighed down by the notion of permanence, intractability, commitment. I wonder if mothers bringing home their babies from the hospital feel like this.

It is a clear, bright day, and it is obvious a snowstorm recently pounded New York City. Mounds of whiteness are shoved aside and soiled. I think of the cold in Siberia. I can conjure it, as though it's been imprinted in my cellular memory. It's as intriguing as everything else was in that place at the end of the world. I fiddle with the radio stations. I land on NPR, but I can't concentrate. I settle on music.

"I'll drop you off in front of the building with the baby and our luggage," Ricky says as we're weaving our way through Central Park to the Upper West Side. "Leave the luggage with Stan. I'll get it after I park."

I want to scream, *No, don't leave me alone with the baby*, but I'm worried Ricky will think I'm a fruitcake. Instead I say, "Maybe you'll get a spot close by and we can walk to the apartment together." We both know that will never happen.

When Ricky does let me out of the car, my knees are wobbling. I need his help extricating Julia from the crazy car seat contraption, then twisting her past the folded-down seat of our two-door car.

"This isn't easy, is it?" I say.

Ricky is huffing. He rips off his wool hat and throws it on the passenger seat. Finally he lifts Julia and hands her to me as though she were a piece of glass. The transfer is awkward because she doesn't seem to have the natural instincts to hold onto my arm or lean close. I had noticed this several times in Moscow when I tried to hold her. It didn't feel the way I thought it would to hold a baby. There was a tension, a resistance. But I didn't think too much about it. Now it gives me pause.

"Okay, I'm going to look for a spot. Good luck," Ricky says, pulling away from the curb. "I love you."

"I love you, too," I say.

What if he never returned? What if I were left alone right now and forever with this brand-new, newborn to me, child who seems as indifferent to me as I still feel for her? It's a terrifying, irrational thought—not too many people perish trying to find a parking spot in Manhattan. But it tells me that my mind is on high panic alert. I'm feeling unsteady. Alien in my new skin. I wonder if Ricky feels like this.

"Oh, my God, Ms. Traster!" says Stan the doorman in his typical staccato speech pattern. "She is absolutely gorgeous." He pulls Julia's snowsuit away from her face to take a better look. "Oh, what a doll she is. Congratulations." Then he pauses. Turns to me and says, "Her eyes. Those are not the eyes of an infant. They are the eyes of a very old soul."

I look at Stan—who Ricky and I secretly call the "former KGB spy" because of his Eastern European accent—and begin to ask him what he means. But then I look at Julia's dark, mysterious eyes, and I suddenly know what he means. It reminds me immediately of the way she grinned at me both times we met at the orphanage. It's as though she learned something about human interaction way too soon, and now I see that in her eyes too. They do not look like an innocent baby's eyes.

“Let me help you,” says Stan, who speaks in clipped sentences and is built like a tank. He holds open the elevator door and presses the button for the eighth floor.

“My husband will get the bags when he comes up,” I say.

Stan is still smiling, standing there like a proud uncle. Come to think of it, he and Julia share physical traits of people from the Eastern bloc. Stan, too, has a large forehead, pale skin, and dark eyes. And of course, he’s a mystery.

I fiddle with the key for a few moments before I can open the door. I’m already envious of those mothers who balance infants on one hip while accomplishing nearly everything else with their other free arm. Our cat comes to see what I’m holding. He sniffs a few times and saunters off. It occurs to me Julia has probably never seen a live animal, not even a dog or a cat.

“Cat,” I say to her. “That’s Floopy, our cat.”

Once inside, I don’t know what to do with myself or with the baby. She probably needs to have her diaper changed or be fed or something obvious, but I lower her into the crib and take off my jacket. I’m hoping Ricky returns quickly, because I know he’ll take charge of the baby. I am overwhelmed and I’m thinking that in any other situation I wouldn’t be. If I walked into the apartment now and there had been a flood, my instincts would kick in and I’d know exactly what to do. But here I am with a baby, my baby, and I am lost.

I hear the elevator doors open and I’m elated.

Ricky walks in the apartment.

“How are my girls?” he says.

I’m amazed at his grace.

“Let me take the baby,” he says. “Let’s get her undressed and bathed and fed,” he says. He’s the one with maternal instincts. But I’m relieved to turn my attention to unpacking, settling in, and making us something to eat.

We are sitting at our round table, which is next to a window that overlooks a courtyard. Steam pours from the radiator. We have put a playpen in between the table and the seating area. The main room of our apartment—the only common room—already feels a lot smaller. Ricky has bathed Julia and dressed her in a onesie. She looks cleaner than I've seen her look yet. She is as bald as a melon. She is sucking on the pacifier we brought from the orphanage. She gurgles as Ricky lowers her into the high chair a cousin donated and ties a bib with a little pig on it around her neck. I'm spreading salad and pasta on the table while he spoon-feeds her organic applesauce. When the jar is empty and he pulls the spoon away for the last time, she cries. Finally. Ricky and I look at each other.

"What should we do? Should we give her another jar?" he asks.

"I don't think so," I say. "She's just getting used to solids. I don't think we should tax her system. How about formula?"

"Okay, let's get that going," he says.

I hand Ricky the bottle. He tips it back into Julia's mouth, and she stops crying.

The pasta has gotten cold. We start eating, but the phone rings.

"That's my mother," I say to Ricky, reminding him that before we left I had arranged for my parents to come over and meet Julia this afternoon.

"Welcome back," my mother says when I answer the phone. "How was the trip? How's the baby?"

"She's good." Ricky's feeding her a bottle. "Are you coming around?"

"Well, there's been a slight change of plans," my mother says, explaining she has my sister's children with her. "I've got Emily and Charlie here with me. They slept over last night. But I'll bring them."

"No!" I shout. "That was not the plan. The plan was for you and Daddy to meet your grandchild this afternoon, alone."

"What's the big deal?" she asks. "We'll all come. Everyone's curious to meet Julia."

"Uh, no, that's not possible," I say.

"What do you mean, why? What's the problem?" she asks, incredulously.

"Julia is not yet allowed to be around other children—she's still too vulnerable," I say, fabricating a ridiculous excuse, as though I was talking about a puppy who couldn't yet go outside because he didn't have his vaccines.

Ricky looks at me queerly.

"I'm sorry, but we had an arrangement and it would be nice if once, just once, you could stick to a plan. I have to go."

I slam down the phone and the tears spill out volcanically. Ah, yes, this is the cry I've been needing. Thanks to my mother, I'm finally having it. Days and days—no, months and months—of building tension, and it took my mother letting me down in order for me to let go. I'm heaving and sobbing and Ricky is rubbing my shoulders.

"You know your mother's not reliable," he says.

"I," *gasp,* "I," *gasp,* "I know, but right now I need a mother," I say. "I wanted this to be special."

Julia watches this scene unfold. She is passive. I'm glad, because I need to be indulged right now.

"She's too vulnerable," Ricky says, starting to laugh. "That's rich. How did you come up with that one?"

I look up at his green eyes, which are alive and twinkling.

Snuffling, I start to laugh too.

"I don't know," I say. "I didn't know what else to say, so I said the first thing that came to my mind."

"Funny," he says. He lifts Julia from the crib and cuddles her.

"You see," he says. "All this fuss is about you."

She gurgles.

He puts her in the playpen.

"Let me clean up. Why don't you sit on the couch and relax?"

Just as I'm sitting down, the phone rings.

"Uh, oh!" I say.

"Hello, Rosalie," Ricky says, answering the phone. "Uh-huh. Uh-huh. I guess that's okay. Okay. See you in a bit."

"What?" I say.

"Your mother says she's going to stop by alone in about a half hour," he says.

I'm tempted to put on my boxing gloves again, but I'm too worn out.

When she knocks on the door, my stomach clenches. She walks into the apartment looking like an Inuit with her big, hooded down jacket and her scarf wrapped around her neck. Her boots are covered with the salt and slush of New York City after a snowstorm. Hunched forward, she makes no effort to take off her coat but carefully takes off her gloves. Then she moves toward Julia with her hands outstretched. I notice her French manicure. My mother bends to look at her but doesn't lift her up because she never lifts anything heavy. She too has a weak back. "Hello," she trills, avoiding eye contact with me entirely. "Oh, she is beautiful."

She still has not removed her coat.

"Would you like a coffee, Rosalie?" Ricky asks.

"Tony and the kids are downstairs in the car waiting for me," she says. "I can't stay long."

I feel like I've been stabbed again. She would have been better off not coming over because at this moment I hate her twice as much.

When she leaves, I curl up on the couch in a ball.

"I just wanted this to be special. To be about Julia and nothing else, not Emily and Charlie. She's been fussing over them forever. She makes me crazy."

"I know, I understand," he says, hesitating. "Maybe this is less important to your mother because Julia is not her own flesh and blood, like Emily and Charlie. Maybe that's not something she's consciously aware of, but maybe her excitement about Julia is tempered because she's adopted. In your mother's eyes, Julia is something *less*."

"You really think that could be the case?" I ask. "I just think she's so angry at me that even giving her a granddaughter is not enough."

"It could be," he says. "Knowing your mother. Forget about Rosalie. She'll come around."

∞∞∞

My mother would say she did the best she could raising me. It would be true. She and my father had a contentious but codependent marriage. She had a master's degree in education from Columbia University; he never finished high school. She was a single child from a coddled Jewish family of Polish immigrants who worked their fingers to the bone at a deli. He was the youngest of six children, a street urchin who had no parental supervision, a good-looking no-goodnik who was a fast thinker and a good dancer. Their worlds collided at a dentist's office. Not too long after, my mother's father died. My father became the man of the household. He lived with my grandmother and mother. It took him four years to marry my mother. I came along in 1962. My sister, Jodie, was born eighteen months later. They built a middle-class life. We lived in a picturesque house in Canarsie. It had rosebushes and a red picnic table in the backyard. They grew a carpet business so successful it paid for trips to Hawaii and Puerto Rico. My father drove a yellow Cadillac. My mother frequently shopped at the jewelers on Rockaway Parkway. There was a lot to protect. So much so that my mother buried her head in the sand when it came to my father's wanderings. I was her favorite child. Her best friend. It was a privilege. It ended up being a burden.

Eight

The next day, Ricky loads up his cart, like Tevye, with tea bags and equipment. He pulls a bungee cord over the merchandise to secure it down. I'd give anything to be the one walking out the door while he stays home with the baby. He kisses me, then Julia, and says, "You'll be fine. Try to enjoy yourself."

I glance over at my desk and think about the work that waits for me. "It will have to sit," I mutter to myself.

Julia is in the playpen. I've noticed she's not too enamored with Elmo and Big Bird. It's strange to have the television on at 9:00 AM. Usually I'm sitting down at my desk now to start my day. My freelance assignments have been coming in regularly again, and I've been grateful for the work. Ricky's working hard at the tea business, but it's still in its infancy.

Julia seems agitated in the crib. I lift her out and dress her. Last night Ricky gave me a diapering lesson. I was thinking, at the time, of my old friend Leah in London. When she gave birth, the government sent home a baby nurse for two weeks, as is the custom for every new mother. What a brilliant idea. Who says any of this stuff is second nature?

Shortly, I will receive my first visitors, if I don't count my mother, which I don't. Jack and Judith are a couple from upstairs. They are my parents' age. We've formed a friendship through our dogs—both of whom have died and are buried side by side in a beautiful cemetery in Westchester. For years we have helped each other out and served as surrogate "dog" parents, and now they are thrilled for Ricky and me as we start our human family.

Judith calls out, "Helloooo!" as she raps on the door.

Julia is in the pen. I think about reaching in and putting her in my arms—the way you might add a broach as an accent at the last minute but then think twice about it—and leave her there.

I open the door.

Judith sails past me.

"Where is the baby girl?"

What is it about babies that makes every woman in her seventies go all sing-songy?

Jack kisses me hello.

"How ya doing?" he asks, genuinely interested.

I think he can see how frazzled I feel.

Judith and Jack hover over the playpen, cooing and clucking.

"Oh, Tina, she's just gorgeous," Judith says.

A birth mother would say "thank you." *What do I say when someone comments on Julia's beauty*?

"Would you like a cup of tea?" I say, leading them to the couch.

I organize tea and cookies, using the lovely Russian teacups I bought in Moscow. *Might as well show off all the beautiful merchandise we brought back*, I think to myself.

When seated and sipping tea, I realize it's hard to make conversation. My relationship with Jack and Judith has always been about mutual helpfulness, so time spent together has always been fleeting moments filled with plans and logistics, not lingering conversations.

"Thanks for coming by," I say, sheepishly.

"Oh, it's our pleasure," Judith trills, maintaining the baby-glow effect. "She's adorable."

Silence.

"So how was the trip?" Jack asks.

He's thrown me a lifeline. I'm comfortable telling stories. I re-create the images of the flat we lived in, whisking Julia away from the orphanage that last night in Novosibirsk. Julia is getting restless.

"Can I hold her?" Judith asks.

"Sure," I say, lifting the baby into Judith's lap.

It seems as though Julia can be handed over to anyone without a fuss.

Judith bobs her on her knee. Julia giggles. I hadn't noticed the dimples near the corner of her mouth before.

She likes the motion.

"Look at the size of her legs," says Judith. Julia squeals with delight.

"I know," I say. "Definitely a future Olympian."

Biting my lip, I decide to tell them about Barbara's meltdown and how ambivalent she was when she met her son.

Judith, who is a psychotherapist, is listening intently, nodding.

When I finish, she says, "Well, sure, many foreign adoptees suffer from Reactive Attachment Disorder. It was a major problem with the Romanian orphans back in the 1980s."

I'm perturbed Judith is so readily familiar with the syndrome. It makes it all the more real. Something I should know about. Or have learned about before we started this process.

"But don't worry," she says. "Julia is young. You got her early, and that's a good thing."

Tension hangs in the room.

"Well, we've got to be going," Jack says.

When they are gone, I look at Julia and wonder if we are going to have trouble bonding. We've been together five days. We are still strangers.

∞∞∞

It's 11:00 AM. The whole day lies before us. I have no plan. Bright sunlight filters through the kitchen window. I eye the stroller near the door.

"C'mon," I whisper to myself. "Millions of mothers do this every day. This can't be brain surgery."

I dress Julia up in warm clothes and the yellow snowsuit. Manipulating the stroller does prove to be an occupational hazard, as though you need some kind of advanced degree to get the thing to stay open. As I struggle I'm worrying about Julia overheating. I think about calling Stan for help, but finally, triumphantly, it kicks into the open position.

"Victory," I say to Julia.

∞∞∞

"How's the little princess this morning?" Stan says, as he greets us at the elevators and bumps the stroller down the three stairs that lead from the lobby to the street.

"Good," I say. "We're going for a walk."

For years and years and years, I'd walk up and down Broadway, romanticizing the image of mother strolling baby. It became an iconic vision in my mind, like baby Jesus and Mary. I always imagined the mother was completely and blissfully at peace while the child gazed around at the milieu of marvels on every sidewalk. I ached to be that mother who felt so at one with herself and her child. In my twenties, I was jet-setting. After my divorce, I was preoccupied with dating and my journalism career. Strolling a baby down the avenue looked like the antidote to my hectic, pressured life.

Here I am, strolling a baby. I am not peaceful. I'm terrified. How does one spend the day with a baby? Will I know for sure when she's hungry? Will she nap? How am I going to juggle caring for her and getting my work done?

As I start walking down Broadway, I realize I have no particular destination. It's brisk outside, and snow is caked up along every curb. At the crosswalks, I struggle to navigate the stroller up onto the sidewalk. People flow by without offering a hand. Julia is not content to sit back and relax. She keeps moving forward in the stroller—almost the reverse action of the back-arching we had seen at the orphanage. I can't figure out if she's uncomfortable or trying to tell me something. I hand her the bottle with formula, which soothes her briefly, but she continues to lean forward and thrust, over and over. After several blocks, I decide to accept that this is what she is going to do, but I keep walking. Eventually Julia falls into a slumber, and I feel the most relief I have felt all day.

Three hours later, I return to our apartment building.

"Oh, my," says Stan. "Looks like someone's cheeks are chafed."

"What? What do you mean?" I say, rushing around to look at Julia under the hood of the stroller.

"Oh, my God," I say, covering my mouth. "What have I done to her?"

"Calm down, Ms. Traster. Her cheeks are just a little red from the wind."

"Oh, my God," I keep saying, embarrassed, mortified, upset.

"I've ruined her," I say, on the verge of tears.

"Ms. Traster. Go put Vaseline on her cheeks. She'll be fine."

We get in the elevator. Julia's face looks like a giant overripe heirloom tomato.

I'm panicking.

How am I going to explain this to Ricky?

Inside, I keep her in the stroller and run to the drawer for Vaseline.

She doesn't appear to be in any sort of discomfort, but she looks freaky. I begin to rub circles of petroleum jelly on each of her cheeks, realizing I should have done this before we went out for a walk on this brisk February day. Julia has not had any exposure to wind or sun or rain. Before we took her from the orphanage, she had never been outside, and when we were in Moscow, we were in and out of cars, driven from one destination to another. Three hours of wind was like a chemical peel for her face.

I take her out of the snowsuit and plunk her in the playpen.

I sit down in the stuffed blue chair, shredded from our cat, and wonder if or when this is going to get easier.

Nine

We are driving down the New Jersey Turnpike on a raw Sunday morning in March. Julia is snuggled in her car seat asleep, her chest rising and falling gently. Her papery eyelids flutter. Finally, some peace for her. For me. For Ricky.

When Julia's awake, she's a constant symphony of sound. Not words, of course, but an ongoing emission of verbal fragments. Her mouth is always open. She is never pensive. She doesn't lounge with a faraway look in her eye. Transitioning from motion to stillness requires relinquishing control, but to do so, Julia would need to fundamentally believe the world is a safe place. Something in her wiring has taught her that relaxing her defenses is dangerous. When I'm in a high state of anxiety, I fear sleep, too. Staying awake tricks me into believing I can ward off danger or control the outcome of whatever is plaguing me simply by turning the issues over in my mind a thousand times. It's a fallacy, but that's how you think when you believe you are alone, that the world is a quickly shifting, unreliable place where bad things happen. I know how *I* got there, but why does my baby behave like that?

It's painful to watch Julia wage a daily battle against rest and relaxation. When I put her down in her crib after lunch, she immediately springs back up and sways back and forth with a crazed look in her eyes. I try to stroke her head or sing to her, but it agitates her. She won't look at me. Eventually I leave her in place to fight it out with herself, and after fifteen to twenty minutes or so, she does succumb, but only because she's out-of-her-head tired.

There's even more drama in the stroller. When she gets groggy, she leans over the stroller's safety bar, the way Kate Winslet does in *Titanic* at the ship's prow, as forward propelling as she can get without doing a flip out of the vehicle. She rattles the bar with her clenched fists as though she is shackled to it, resisting the pull of sleep.

But the car is another story. The vibration and continuous movement, especially when we're driving on the highway, is as irresistible as an undertow at sea. She bangs her head against her car seat to keep herself awake, but it's futile. The motion is hypnotic. Her head flops onto her shoulder or forward onto her chest. She's transported, but to where? Does she dream? Do people in her dreams speak Russian? Is she back in the orphanage where it smells like ammonia and cooked cabbage? Perhaps she's in the comfort of one of her caretaker's arms, someone whose scent is more familiar?

She looks peaceful. Beautiful, really. She usually rests for exactly one hour, like clockwork, as though she's been rigged like a bomb waiting to go off. She does not whimper or fuss or appear to be in discomfort. But then, like a scene in a horror movie, she will wake as though someone were coming at her with a gleaming knife. Or she's seen a ghost, which perhaps she has.

Ricky has a theory about why this happens. He thinks when she's asleep, she slips back to her early days in the orphanage, and when she comes to from napping, she has no idea where she is or who we are. She's in an unsettling state of disorientation, a fugue.

We're still motoring along the turnpike, fifty minutes into her nap, when I get the Pavlovian stomach clench, knowing she'll wake in ten minutes. I lower the radio and twist around toward her. I extend my arm and cup my hand around her knee, hoping the warmth and pressure might make her feel more grounded and secure. She stirs. I hold my breath and stand ready with a bottle of formula in my other hand. Her eyes bat quickly. She crinkles her brow and then, on cue, she emits a keening howl. "It's okay," I coo. "It's okay. You're here with Mommy and

Daddy. Here's your bottle." If that doesn't work, I offer her the *abaye*, the mysterious word she uses for her pacifier. Either way, her eyes never meet mine. Today, she takes the formula from me and sucks down every last drop of liquid like a desert-thirsty nomad. Then she tosses the empty bottle beside her on the seat. She sits up tall and strikes up her one-man band of sing-song sound.

"We'll be there soon," I say, guessing my words, or the assuring tone, mean nothing.

I shift back around in the passenger seat. Ricky can sense my discomfort.

"You okay?" he asks.

"Yeah, you know, I don't know," I say. Then I add in a hushed voice, "She's *so* not at peace. It's upsetting."

"She'll get there," he says. "She just needs time."

"Maybe, but that spooked look in her eyes worries me."

Ricky puts his hand on my knee, and I lean back and close my eyes. What a gift it is to receive comfort from another person. My mind drifts and I think about something that happened a few days ago in the playground.

It was a dank, dull day like this one, but I was going stir-crazy in the apartment and couldn't stand the thought of another trip down Broadway to Barnes & Noble. I bundled Julia into a snowsuit, and we set off to Riverside Park. This was both mine and Julia's maiden voyage to a playground. I'd been to the Hudson River park countless times but never to the part with the swings and slides and jungle gyms. I don't recall seeing a playground at the orphanage, and if there was one, Julia would have been too young to have seen it. I felt a mixture of hope and fear bubbling in my chest. I left the building and walked toward the river. At the entrance, I bumped the stroller down a set of massive stone steps and looked around. It was desolate. The sky was flat. I could see joggers in the distance against the backdrop of the roiling silver river and a few scattered homeless people piled under ragged woolen coats on benches, but Julia and I were the only souls on the playground. A chill coursed through me, but I resisted the urge to turn back. It wasn't snowing or raining or terribly windy; what could be the harm of giving this a go? I parked the stroller at the base of the metal slide and wrestled Julia in her bulky snowsuit out of the belted contraption. I lifted her as high as I could midway up the slide and eased her down with a big, squeaky "wheeeeeeeeeeeeeee." She was agreeable, so I repeated this exercise a few times. Then I looked around thinking, *okay, what else?*

The climbing equipment looked too daunting for a baby, so I turned in the other direction where I noticed two hulking behemoths with long horns. "Look, Julia, din-o-saur. Look at the big din-o-saurs. Ooh, you can climb on those." I trotted over to the beasts and propped her up on one of the creatures' back. Then I pulled her along its sloping tail. She seemed pleased. On the third excursion I said aloud, "Dinosaurs are extinct. They don't live on earth anymore. But they used to." She looked at me blankly. I suppose any baby would. There are times when you hear yourself talking and it catches you by surprise. I have just told my child that dinosaurs no longer live on earth. There's no part of that idea she can absorb now, and yet it seemed like the right thing to say. I planted the idea like a seed, knowing one day it will have meaning. And then I thought, *Right! That's what it takes.* Nurture doesn't necessarily show its benefit right away, but if you keep planting seeds, they are bound to take root. Given enough time and experience, Julia will learn to trust. Napping won't be scary. I won't be a stranger.

"Okay, let's try the swings."

I carried her to the row of the little boxy swings. I hoisted her in one, with a moan because she's heavy as a sack of potatoes, and threaded her little feet through the holes to let her legs dangle. I walked behind the idling swing and gave it a gentle puff of a push. With no warning, she released a blood-curdling scream. I ran back to the front of the swing, stopping it immediately, thinking I didn't have her in the seat correctly. I looked around to figure out what was wrong, but nothing was obvious. I smelled her bottom. She was clean. She had the queerest look of terror on her face. I returned to the back of the swing, and again, gave it a wee nudge. This time she wailed even louder. I fumbled again to the front of the swing and wriggled her from the seat. "Okay, okay, no swing, no swing!" and in an instant, she was fine. She stopped crying; it was like nothing had ever happened, like a button had been turned off. But when I pulled her toward me to comfort her and tell her that I was sorry, she instinctively flexed her muscles to deflect me.

I put her back into the stroller and trudged uphill back to the apartment, stunned. What had just happened? What baby doesn't like a gently swaying swing? I always thought children are in thrall when they swing. Even adults like to shoehorn their bottoms into a malleable rubber swing and take a ride down memory lane. I kept thinking about the sensation of being on a swing. It's a way to lose yourself. Then, in a flash, I realized something. Abandoning control is the last thing in the world Julia wants. Being suspended in a little chair, high above the ground with someone arbitrarily pushing you from behind is tantamount to torture. There's no way to resist or brace herself, the way she does in the stroller. What she must have felt was the panic of a free fall, the absolute loss of whatever control she constantly fights for.

At home, I changed her diaper and slotted her into her high chair. I shook some raisins onto her tray, then grabbed a jar of Earth's Best baby food. I tried to feed her, but she wanted to feed herself. She's been doing that more and more. I watched her closely, analyzing my mysterious child. She's not daunted by the high chair, which is also confining and high off the ground, but she can see the ground and there's no motion. I gazed at her face for a moment and inhaled a deep, heavy breath. After lunch, I put Julia in her crib for a nap, and though she struggled, the excitement of the day took her under. I tiptoed into the other room and called Ricky.

"The weirdest thing just happened," I said.

"What was it? Everything okay?"

"Yeah, we're fine, I think. I took Julia to the park, to the playground."

"It wasn't too cold?"

"No, that wasn't an issue. I put her on the slide and the dinosaur."

"The what?"

"There's this dino—never mind. Just listen. When I put her in the swing, she freaked out. I mean freaked out like you've never seen."

"How so?"

"She howled, like she was being attacked," I said.

"Maybe she was hungry or cold or wet?" he said.

"No, it wasn't that. She reacted viscerally to the motion of the swing. She was fine before and fine the second I extricated her," I said. "But she couldn't stand being in that swing when it was moving."

"Well, don't put too much stock in it," he said. "There are a lot of things that don't feel natural to her because she's never experienced them before. One day she'll love swings."

"And me? Will she love me one day?"

"What?"

"I'll call you later."

We are riding along the final section of the New Jersey Turnpike to a friend's party in Pennsylvania. This ribbon of road is a vessel of memories. In 1992, I took a job as a reporter at a daily newspaper in New Jersey. I worked the late shift, more than an hour from my apartment. My marriage was disintegrating. My career sustained me. A decade has passed, but the turnpike churns up those days. The most vivid memory I have is working on a story about Gail Shollar. She was a thirty-four-year-old mother, walking with her three-year-old from a food store to her car in a shopping center parking lot. She was carrying groceries in one hand and holding her daughter's hand with the other. A man with a gun crept up behind her and forced her and her toddler into her car. The next day, her toddler had been found, cold and crying, dumped in front of a day care center. Four days later I was deployed by my editor to a drainage ditch behind a local lumberyard where I waited a couple of hours before police recovered the mother's raped and stabbed body from a ditch. For months, I could feel Gail Shollar's spirit. I'd picture her on that night, in her car, a prisoner, unable to protect herself and her baby. I was haunted by the thought of the small child's confusion. Her mother was powerless to protect her. And the panic that child must have felt after being tossed onto the unfamiliar street. It was unbearable to contemplate. The man who committed this heinous act was caught, but what lingered was the sadness of a little girl who would always carry the memory of having her mother snatched from her and of a mother who knew she was defenseless to help her little girl.

When I can't come to Julia's rescue, I suffer.

Ten

Julia is popping up and down in her playpen like a Whac-a-Mole, but she's not playing a game with me. She's not trying to catch my eye to play peek-a-boo. She's not looking for her "up" to complete my "down." She's in her own world, in motion, as always. She needs to move, flex, push, pull, rock, shake, rearrange. She has a burning desire to break beyond whatever is physically binding her. When she's not busting out, she busies herself, like an officious secretary in a hectic office. People who meet her ask me if she ever stops moving, if she ever relaxes. I say no to both questions. She's on a perpetual mission of motion.

Is she trying to stay one step ahead of a ghost?

Her manic behavior reminds me of my mother. My mother is and has always been terrified of what I call white space. Everything needs to be filled in. Schedules and appointments paper the day. A Saturday night without plans gives her an anxiety attack. She needs a list of things to do, a list she never effectively tackles. Her bag bulges with scraps of paper filled with names and numbers of people she needs to call and make an appointment with. There are stacks of magazines in her apartment she will never read. She can't take twenty minutes and sit in her plant-filled living room with its wraparound windows and enjoy a quiet moment. She moves from one thing to the next, as she always has. I can't recall her idling on a bench or staring out the window. Call her and she'll ask you to hold on seven times while she takes other calls, feeds the dogs, and nudges my father to go down the hall and collect the laundry. Sit with her and try to have a conversation. Impossible. Practiced distraction was the salve that helped her avoid her painful marriage. Rather than think, she did. She worked, drove, arranged, manned phones, did paperwork, helped with homework, supervised my father, ran to the beauty parlor, and then collapsed into bed at night with a book that lay open on her slow-rising and falling chest as she drifted off to sleep. I don't know if she ever finished a book. She skimmed a lot.

In my childhood home, we had a pair of crushed-velvet burnt-orange love seats in the living room. When I left for college, the cushions were as new as they had been the day they had been delivered thirteen years earlier. We didn't sit around. We didn't watch television. There was no television. We remained busy from sunup to sundown. Productivity was a way of life, an *ism*. My inclination, too, was to fill white space by reading, doing projects, practicing the piano, or preparing for a dance recital. As an adult, I was afraid to be alone with my thoughts, to face a blank calendar. My divorce, the blessedly apocalyptic moment where I reevaluated virtually everything, offered up a chance for change. I had to learn to be still. I finally understood that constant so-called productivity was really a tactic for avoidance. Rather than date right away, I allowed myself to grieve my lost marriage. I learned to hear my voice, to listen to desires that had been repressed. I pushed my mother's voice out of my head, until it went away permanently. I taught myself to balance fruitful time with time-outs. I took baths. I did yoga. I sought out white space. I remembered how to daydream again. I was not afraid to be alone.

Julia's only a baby, but I worry she is afraid to be. To just be. Sometimes I think she moves around and verbalizes nonstop as a way of telling herself she is there. I wish I could soothe her so she'd be free to daydream.

∞∞∞

Today Julia and I have music class at 11:00 AM. Mothers, nannies, and occasionally a father bring babies nine to fifteen months old. We gather in a large circle around a chipper troubadour who nests in our enclosure.

He has a skinned drum, a flute, a tambourine, and a guitar. It's kiddie Kumbaya. This will be the third mommy-and-me music class I try with Julia. The idea is to spend time sitting on the rim of the circle, bonding with your baby through music. Seems simple enough. Mommy holds baby up and wiggles her to the tune of the music. Baby smiles, sways, shows delight. Endorphins course the veins. Over the span of forty-five minutes, the troubadour mixes up the music with drum beating, and he teaches simple hand motions to go along with the songs. All very simple, except Julia refuses to participate. She will not let me hold her up so she can move to the rhythm. She won't even remain in the circle. As soon as we settle in, she takes off on her knees—and at ten months old, it seems incorrect to say she's "crawling." She's a Ferrari on knees, a caterpillar on steroids. I can barely keep up with her. She uses raw determination to scud across the large gym floor. There's a lot of territory in here and dangerous equipment, so I go in chase, again and again.

The weirdest part is that she gets far ahead of me, gaining such distance that she can't even see me, nor does she bother to look back. This doesn't panic her. In the orphanage she learned that someone will eventually come along, pluck her up, and put her back in a crib or a high chair or another depot of sorts. It didn't—and perhaps still doesn't—matter who that is. She has no built-in notion that mother and child should be within reach of one another.

I can't figure out why Julia is so disinterested in an activity like this. Other babies wander a little here and there, but only she goes AWOL. She's not deaf, I'm certain of that, so it's not that she doesn't hear the music. Music is a universal language, so it's not a language issue. I leave again today feeling deflated because we have missed another opportunity to do something that might make us feel closer. In my darkest moments, I believe her behavior is intentional, that Julia simply won't allow intimate moments to flower, though I cannot fathom why. Then I tell myself, *That's ridiculous*, but I'm lying to myself. My gut reaction is right. Something is wrong.

I've been at this mothering thing for three months. It's only to myself that I admit I dislike it most of the time. Contrary to what I expected,

I'm not experiencing any bliss. I'm not lost in love or swept up in rapture. I'm bored, restless. I don't look forward to the days; I get through them. Having work and deadlines on my mind constantly and trying to squeeze in what I can when I can, doesn't help, but I don't think that's the real problem. Enough time has gone by that I feel bereft. What if Julia and I never bond? What if I never feel deep love for her? Sometimes my mind plays a terrible game. If she were in perilous danger, would I save her if I knew I'd be risking my own life? I don't know.

The other day I was walking up and down Broadway strolling Julia. I thought back to the scene outside the courtroom when we finalized the adoption. Olga was prepping us, as she always did before any official interaction. She said the judge would ask a few questions, she'd interpret them, and we'd respond. They were simple basic questions, but she made a point to say, "If the judge asks who will care for the baby, tell her you will be home with the baby full time." She said this with her eyes boring into mine. Then she knitted her brow and said, "Do not tell her the baby will have a nanny or go to day care."

"Of course," I had said.

In fact I hadn't planned any kind of day care or nanny. I hadn't planned anything at all. When we were called back to Russia to finalize the adoption so swiftly, time stopped. I turned my attention to returning to Siberia and preparing the apartment and Julia's nursery for her homecoming. I could only project far enough to dream of the day we'd arrive at Kennedy Airport with our baby. I'm realizing I need to hire someone so I can free up some of my time. I need balance, and whether that's frowned upon by the Russians or by other mothers, so be it. I need to face down my biggest critic: me.

The next day, en route to a new mommy-and-me experiment, I stop at the health food store and hang a flier that says I'm looking for someone to care for Julia three hours every morning. I tack it up on the board and whisper to myself, "Gotta do this."

We continue walking down Broadway in the April morning sunshine. The dogwoods are blooming. I feel a little brighter than I usually do. Julia and I arrive at a brownstone where we leave the stroller on the ground floor with a fleet of other strollers. I carry Julia up one flight to the classroom. I'd read about mommy-and-me yoga and thought maybe, just maybe, this might work.

Ten mats are staggered across the studio's hardwood floor. Light pours through large windows, casting angular shadows. Mothers sit on mats, coddling and nuzzling their babies. Babies gurgle with delight. It's as though you can enter the room only if you and your baby are a Hallmark moment. One woman and her child look like a Madonna and Child sculpture. The babies are propped on their mothers' knees or draped over their mothers' stomachs as though straddling a rocking horse. The babies are bounced and stroked and loved all over. It's like a maternity ward, umbilical cords intact. There's no chaos or crying. What kingdom have I entered?

Please let this work. Please let this work. I offer a silent prayer to the yogi gods, aware I'm fragile and tired and hoping I'll receive manna this morning. I remove Julia's little wool sweater and her shoes. Mine are already off. There's an empty mat in the second row. Women perched around me offer beatific smiles. I sit down while holding onto Julia's chubby arm. When I'm situated on the floor, I pull her toward me. I try to imitate the other women. Some are sitting with their legs open in a *V* and stretched out. Their babies are squeezed in the crook made by the formation of the *V.* I try to assume this position, using all my might to pull Julia into place. The more I try to keep her next to me, the more she pulls away. The band of tension between us is palpable. This is no way to prepare for yoga. *Deep breath. Deep breath.*

In wafts a waif wearing a bun and a dreamy expression. She probably doesn't have children. Setting down CDs, she stretches both sides of her lithe body and takes a few deep breaths.

"Good morning all," she whispers, bowing her head. "What a beautiful morning."

Julia's forcefulness strains my arms. If I hold her more tightly, I'm afraid someone will call child services.

I release the pressure, and she takes off on her knees across the room.

The waif sniffs the air.

"Sorry," I say, quickly sprinting after her. The room is small, so she can't get beyond my sight. I scoop her up and take her back to the mat. Just as she won't stay close, neither does she resist being brought back to home base.

"Okay, let us begin. Let's sit opposite our babies."

"Om. Ommm. Ommmmm."

While the rest of the room is in freakishly perfect order, Julia and I are fumbling. This isn't mommy-and-me yoga. It's mommy-and-me wrestling. I situate her opposite me. I'm supposed to stretch up and around her to embrace her. She, in turn, is supposed to enjoy the nurture. But by the time I reach forward, she's back on her knees, pointed toward the CD player. My heart flutters as she heads for the CD player, with all its shiny buttons. Fearful she'll disrupt the perfect harmony, I leap up and snatch her. The waif avoids my eyes.

Now the mothers are being instructed to massage their babies. I put my hands on Julia's powerful legs and squeeze. I glance around to see other babies lying prostrate on the floor, enjoying the physical contact. Julia whips around and she's back on her knees again. "It's no use," I say, audibly. A mother in the front row looks over her shoulder with a compassionate expression. *Sure,* I think to myself. *You look at me like that. What do* you *know? Or you? Or you? Or any of you with your babies and your perfect mother world?* I realize I'm on the brink of tears or maybe a nervous breakdown. I've got to get out of this room. I can't take another minute of this humiliation. I grab Julia, carry her downstairs, and put her in the stroller.

"Why is everything so difficult with you?" I bark. In the height of my upset and disillusionment, I notice something important. Julia does not appear to be upset even though I'm so clearly unhinged. There's no look of concern or fear in her eyes. Is this normal? I realize babies are egocentric, but if their mother, or even a constant caretaker, which is what I imagine Julia thinks I am, is having a meltdown, wouldn't that jar a healthy baby?

At that moment, I stop pitying myself. A tremendous shroud of sadness for Julia envelops me. My heart aches for her. How alone she must be. How alone I feel. We're two unfortunate souls who've come together, both needing love yet each unable to help the other. As I walk home, I have my true yoga moment. I realize the universe—if one is to believe in something divine—has put us together to work through something complicated and powerful. I don't know exactly what it is yet, but there, on the sunny spring street, I accept that Julia has come to me for a reason.

Eleven

Lurnie arrives at 9:30 Monday morning, thirty minutes late. Stan, the doorman, gave me her number. She babysits other children in our building. I hired her to look after Julia while I work from 9:00 to noon, weekdays. She seemed affable and soft-spoken, almost hypnotic because of her Jamaican lilt. Her mild manner might suit Julia. I'm a stickler for time. I try not to show my displeasure when she shows up late. She enters the apartment with a toothy grin and lunges playfully toward Julia, arms wide open for a hug.

Lurnie and I have discussed my expectations. I need her to mind Julia inside the apartment but to stay as far away as possible from the desk where I'm on the telephone working. Lurnie was understandably perplexed when I told her I didn't want her to take Julia outside the apartment. I had said, "I know it's a weird request, but we recently adopted Julia and I'm still, you know, getting used to . . . " She stopped me there, squeezed my forearm, and said, "I completely understand." That's what made me hire her.

Newspaper reporters learn to focus in a fog of noise. Editors shout, televisions blare, phones ring, reporters converse on the phones. To write or think, you go into a long tunnel. The world around you dims. You've got a deadline. That's all there is. I'm hoping that training is going to work with this new arrangement because the apartment is only so big.

⚮⚮⚮

For the next few weeks, I resume something of a work routine while Lurnie and Julia cavort in every square inch of the apartment. By the end of May, Lurnie's timekeeping is deteriorating. She shows up at 10:00 AM, 10:30 AM, sometimes not at all. Every day I wake with a knotted stomach, wondering how much of my day will be chipped away by her tardiness. It's harder to eat breakfast. When she does show up, I'm less and less sunny. It doesn't occur to me there are a thousand Lurnies who need the work. Everything about my existence seems so vulnerable.

That next day I told Lurnie it was time to take Julia outside. First for one hour, then two, and then we'd work up to the whole morning. Lurnie looked relieved. Julia showed no look of concern when they left the apartment together for the first time. Finally having time, and the apartment, completely to myself was a relief, yet I can't say I was at ease. Although I don't feel a blissed-out, endorphin-pumping mother's love when I'm with Julia, I'm also not at ease when I'm not with her. I feel the weight of her preciousness, like she's irreplaceable, and that's literally true. She can't be replaced, and I can't *have* another kid. We couldn't *afford* to adopt another child. There are no second chances.

⚮⚮⚮

For a few weeks, a new rhythm takes hold. I am more balanced and productive. Then Lurnie becomes even less reliable. It's not unusual for her to be a no-show, for her to not even call. One dreary Wednesday is such a day. I'm particularly annoyed because in addition to revising a story that's been sent back to me by an impatient editor, I want to finish last-minute arrangements for a party we're throwing on Saturday. It's Julia's "coming-out" party. Ricky made great invitations for fifty guests. The card had a stork carrying a baby, and he Photoshopped the word "Aeroflot" on the stork. I bought Julia a special dress. We've been very excited to introduce Julia to our world.

I've got to talk to Ricky's mother, who's agreed to cater the party. I need to make some calls to follow up with people who have yet to RSVP. Ricky's put together a CD track, and he bought *Fiddler on the Roof* to give the party a hint of Russian-ness.

I blow my lips in frustration and mumble, "I just can't rely on anyone." Julia is crawling around the apartment, dragging books from her room to the living room, not to read but to rearrange.

"Now what?"

I lift Julia onto the changing table and put on a fresh diaper. "We can dress later," I say. "Let's see what I can wear to your party," I say, guiding her to the bedroom by holding her outstretched arms while she toddles wobbily. She'll be walking in a few weeks. I lift her up and plop her on my bed. She throws herself on top of the cat, who instinctively seems to know not to harm her. But I pull Julia back and show her how to pet the cat more gently.

I hesitate for a moment, then walk three feet across the room to a bureau of drawers. Just as I bend down to pull open a dresser drawer, I hear a thud that paralyzes my body. Before I whip around, I know the bed is going to be empty, but I cannot believe it when I see her on the hardwood floor. She's lying next to the leg of the wrought-iron bed, and she's silent. I scream and lunge to get her. By the time I do, she is wailing. There are no cuts or bleeding, but she's more inconsolable than I've ever seen her. A hideous purple blot is spreading along her left temple, like wet ink. I hold her tighter than I ever have. *Oh my God, oh my God, what have I done? What is the matter with me? How could I have turned my back for a second while she was sitting on our tall queen bed? Oh my God, what have I done?* I hug and hug her. Her crying subsides. My leaden legs slog toward the kitchen. I bend sideways into the freezer and extract ice cubes, which I wrap in a dishtowel. She fusses when I press cold compresses against her temple. *Oh my God, what have I done? I could have killed her.* I'm dizzy. I feel like I'm going to throw up. Time has stopped.

Deep breaths. Deep breaths. You're the adult. You're the mother. She needs you to remain levelheaded. I reach for the phone and hit speed dial for the pediatrician.

Hysterically I tell the receptionist I have an emergency. She puts a nurse on the phone. I start rambling, but she stops me. She's asking the questions. Yes, the baby cried. No, she didn't pass out. Yes, she seems alert. No, she didn't vomit. The nurse makes order of chaos. An angel at a dark moment. Julia's vital signs seem okay. The nurse doesn't recommend a visit to the emergency room, though she tells me to watch for a series of signs that might indicate a concussion.

I've got Julia on my lap, but now she's done crying and appears ready to resume her busyness. She eats a rice cracker. The eggplant-shaded bruise is an abomination. It broadcasts to the world I'm not bonded enough to my baby to know that leaving her on a tall, queen-size bed is a stupid, careless idea.

I have no choice but to soothe myself. The nurse said it sounded like it wasn't a critical fall. All the vital signs are there. *Breathe. Breathe.* I can hardly breathe.

Then it hits me.

Oh my God. What am I going to tell Ricky?

I have never lied to my husband. I have an unnatural need to keep everything in sunlight. That's not his nature, but over time, that's the way we've become together. But for the first time I know I'm going to lie by omission. I'm going to tell him she's taken a fall, but I'm going to say she ran into the bed leg. I can't bring myself to say I turned my back on her while she was on the bed. It's not that he'll chastise me; in fact, it's the opposite. He'll be patient and understanding and tell me every new mother makes a mistake or two and that I'm being too harsh with myself.

I run down the conversation with the nurse, point by point. He listens calmly. He believes I have the situation under control. Maybe I do. He says he'll call in a couple of hours to check in. I put down the phone and stare at the baby, who is piling stuffed animals into a toy stroller. It's amazing. She's fallen, got hurt, been soothed, moved on. But that purple blotch taunts me. It's a warning. *You got a pass this time. Count yourself lucky.*

I look skyward and thank whoever it is who watches over.

But as I glance back at Julia, my stomach clenches.

Oh my God. What are we going to do about your party? How can I introduce you to the world with a neon sign that says, "Bad mommy"?

I call Ricky back.

"What's the matter?" he says, alarmed.

"No, nothing, but what are we going to do about Saturday?"

"What do you mean?"

"Julia looks terrible. How can we . . . ?"

"Don't worry. Babies heal quickly. We've got five days before the party."

"Are you sure? Should we cancel?"

"I don't think so. All the arrangements are made. Everyone is coming. Try to calm down. Maybe go for a walk with Julia, if she's okay. If you're okay."

"You're right. I've got to get out of here. I've also got to get a more reliable babysitter. I have to get rid of Lurnie."

"Look. You're upset. Try not to focus on a million things. Take a walk. Keep an eye on Julia. I'm sure she's fine."

I dress Julia and negotiate her into the stroller. What was I thinking? I should know she has no sense of boundaries. As we start down the street, I recall a telephone conversation I'd had a few weeks ago with our adoption counselor. She called because we hadn't filed a written post-adoption report, which we are supposed to do every six months. I wasn't particularly apologetic because I resent the agency's continued involvement in our life. Still, I agreed to give an oral report. The questions were basic. Yes, Julia was eating, gaining weight, meeting milestones. I told them I could see she'd be walking soon. Yes, she was a good sleeper. Of course, I'd said we're all very happy. Then, an odd question. "Does she recognize danger?" Of course, I'd whipped out, not thinking twice about the question. After I hung up with the counselor, I wondered what she meant. *Does she recognize danger?* The more I thought about it, the more I realized I wasn't sure I'd given an honest answer. Julia crawls away from me without any concern as to my whereabouts. She thrusts toward any cat or dog she encounters. She hesitates at nothing. In Julia's mind, it didn't occur to her that the edge of the bed was a cliff.

It's a long afternoon before Ricky comes home. When Julia naps, I'm scared she won't wake up. I check obsessively to make sure she's breathing. I feel her skin for fever, but she's cool. Her eyes aren't glazed. After I feed her lunch I'm afraid she'll vomit, but she doesn't. If she had died it would have been my fault. I'm racked with guilt. My confidence is shattered.

I have seen babies left on parents' beds before, surrounded by a barricade of pillows. Those babies don't roll off. Why? Something occurs to me. Other babies sleep in bed with their parents. The bed is a place where they've been breast-fed, lulled to sleep, coddled. Julia has never spent a night in our bed. She's a good sleeper, and Ricky and I agree we want to keep our bed a marital bed and not make it a family bed.

The sound of Ricky's key jiggling the lock is music.

I run into his arms and convulse.

"It's all right," he says, stroking my hair. "Where is she?"

He walks to the playpen and brushes his hand gently along her purple forehead.

"Wow. That's a shiner."

I avoid his eye.

"We could call her Gorbachev," he says.

It's Saturday. We are preparing for the party. Julia has been fine. The bruise is a lighter shade of gray and not as pervasive as it was at first. Ricky comes into Julia's nursery while I'm slipping a floral sundress carefully over her head.

He looks at me intently.

"She's fine. It'll be fine. Every baby has taken a spill at one time or another."

I know he's right, but still.

Ricky just got off the phone with his mother. She and my mother are in the party room in my parents' building, setting up the food and drinks. He is going to head over with balloons, and I'll catch up in forty minutes.

"Take Julia. I'll meet you there."

Everything is festively arranged when I arrive. My mother says hello, but we don't kiss or embrace. "I've got something for Julia," she says, pointing to some shopping bags in the corner of the room.

"Thanks," I say, sweeping past her to say hello to Ricky's mother and then to the guests who are streaming into the room. I'm on guard, holding my breath, waiting for someone to ask what happened to Julia. No one does. Seems conspiratorial.

"Ricky, look, it's Robert and his wife," I say.

We have not seen Robert, Laura, or Noa since the day we left Moscow on the Orphan Express with our babies. Noa is fourteen months and walking. She's a beautiful child, with a shock of long, silky black hair. Although Laura is white and Jewish, she too has a long, exotic mane that somehow makes her look like Noa, even though the child is of Muslim descent. Robert and I hug in a long embrace. Laura brushes past my cheek with an air kiss. Noa paws at Robert's pants; she wants to see Julia. I bend down and put the babies side by side, though Noa looks more like a toddler. Ricky says hello, too. He takes Julia from me, and he and Laura break into a side conversation.

"So, how are you doing?" Robert asks with deep chocolate eyes and a crinkled brow.

"I'm okay. I'm, uh, good. How are you?"

He rolls his eyes.

"What a life-changing experience," he says. "I remember the day we were in the visa office together. God, that seems like a lifetime ago."

"It was," I say.

"Are you and Rick happy? Have things been going well?"

"As you say, the whole thing is life-changing. I'd say overwhelming."

"I know what you mean. It's hard when you're an older parent. You've got a whole lifetime behind you, and then suddenly you have to be, you know, that life isn't yours anymore."

"I know exactly what you mean," I say, feeling lighter, for a change. "I wasn't totally prepared for this."

"Yeah, but hey, what's the choice? You gotta go with it? No?"

"You are right," I say. "Come, have something to eat."

A conversation with a squeak of honesty. Refreshing.

I move through a sea of people. Everyone is having fun. *Fiddler* has gone around a couple of times. The food table is pilfered. The wine bottles are empty. The babies are groggy. We are saying good-bye. So many promises to do this or that. So many "Congratulations."

Light is falling as we stroll with Julia north along Broadway to our apartment.

"It went well," Ricky says. "Good job."

"I think everyone enjoyed themselves. Julia was a big hit," I say.

"Many people remarked on how beautiful she is," he says.

I look at Ricky with a *C'mon* look.

"What?"

"No one said anything? Not one person asked about the bruise on her head? You must have sent a communiqué telling people to stay mum, no?"

"Yes, that's what I did."

"I thought so."

We laugh, and he plants a kiss on my lips.

Twelve

I am sitting on a plush couch in a communal lounge on the top floor of my mother's condo waiting to meet two Upper West Side mothers and their children. Julia, dressed in lightweight, geometrically patterned pants and a matching T-shirt, barrels between the bookshelves and the television before heading to the floor-to-ceiling windows. After finding these women on an Internet chat site, I've been communicating with Jen and Nancy by e-mail for the past couple of weeks. I'm especially excited to meet Nancy, who has recently returned from Kazakhstan with her adopted daughter.

Jen arrives first. She is all freckles and a wild mane of auburn hair. Her little boy, Jason, is slumped over in his stroller, napping. Jen sweeps into the room and extends a hand to introduce herself. I invite her to take a seat and say, "That's Julia," pointing to the far corner of the room. Julia doesn't look up or acknowledge us. We are chatting for less than ten minutes when Jason begins stirring. He rubs his eyes and seeks Jen's attention. "Hello, Angel," she hums, lowering her face two inches from his. "Hungry?" she asks. She lifts the fleshy baby out of the stroller, opens her blouse, and brings him to her breast. He suckles contentedly.

"Are you breast-feeding?" she asks.

Before I can answer, I notice a looming figure in the doorway. This must be Nancy, and though she is under five feet, she looks like a giant because she's carting a baby in a large knapsack. I greet her and lead her to the couch where we are sitting. Jen, still feeding, says hello. Then Jen reaches into her cavernous bag and tosses toys and a large rubber ball onto the floor. It had never occurred to me to bring toys. Jason, still clutching his mother, entwining himself in her hair, is not interested in the little trucks or the puzzles, but Julia makes a beeline for the red and white rubber ball and snatches it. She throws it in front of her and chases it, again and again.

"Wow," says Jen. "She's a powerhouse."

Meanwhile, Nancy is unpacking her baby, Vera. Vera is thirteen months, two months older than Jason and Julia. Nancy hands her shoes to put on her feet, but Vera holds up the shoes to Nancy's face and Nancy puts them on for her. Immediately, Vera lunges for the ball in Julia's hands and snags it. Julia does not put up a fuss. She has no "that's mine" reflex. She just moves on to other toys strewn on the carpet. I watch this curiously, because we have not been around other babies that much. But I have noticed time and again that Julia never puts up a fight when another child takes something from her. On the other hand, I have never seen her commandeer something another child is holding or playing with.

Nancy, forty-seven, is an animated pixie. After our introduction, she jumps right into her story about having spent a month in Kazakhstan before she and her husband, Dennis, could bring Vera home. Like Ricky and I, she and her husband are older, first-time parents.

"So tell me about your experience in Russia," she says, smiling at me, then at Julia.

I shift my attention to Jen, realizing I'd left her question about breastfeeding hanging.

"Julia is also adopted." I say to her.

While I talk about our adventures in Siberia, Jason grows more animated, though at eleven months, he appears to be behind the two little girls. Jen says he's not walking yet. Vera is spinning around the room like a tornado. I recognize her manic energy. It's the same behavior I see in Julia, moving this way, then that, here and there, eyes darting, scrambling, climbing up, climbing down, unable to sit still. But there's one difference. Although Julia takes off like a rocket into space and leaves me behind, Vera is like a planet circling a star. She's back at Nancy every few minutes, seeking attention. She clings to her. Doesn't let her speak. She puts her face right up close to Nancy's.

"Go on, Vera, go play with Julia."

Vera runs to Julia with an impish grin and takes the remote Julia's examining in her hand. She tears off across the room with maniacal peals of laughter.

"It's okay," I say to Nancy. "Julia will find something else to play with."

Nancy looks surprised. I imagine she's accustomed to a mother getting up to console a child who's just had something snatched from her hand, but I know it won't faze Julia and it doesn't.

We spend the next hour getting to know one another. We agree to meet in a week's time in the park and to recruit other mothers and their babies. On my walk back home, I replay in my mind what I'd witnessed, as I always do when I'm around other mothers and their babies. While Jason sought his mother's attention in a passive way, Vera used all her energy and wiles to engage her mother relentlessly. In both cases, Jen and Nancy were distracted, constantly tending to their children. Julia is so self-contained, I'm less needed.

The playgroup sprouts like fungal mushrooms in a marshy meadow. By August, we have a dozen mothers and their babies, most around eleven months old. We meet once or twice a week in the playground or spread a quilt of mismatched blankets in the park where we while away long, hot summer days.

To the unknowing eye, Julia is not particularly different from other children—at least not on the surface. She is walking, she has as much hair and as many teeth. She is stringing together words to make sentences. But there's one glaring difference between Julia and the others: Vera and Jason and Jane and Jack express a range of moods and emotions.

On one day, a child is cranky or clingy; on another, he's perky, more exploratory. Julia has one consistent demeanor. She's always cheerful, exuberant, active. The mothers constantly remark that she's the happiest child they've ever encountered. She doesn't complain. She never throws a tantrum. I'd like to believe the mothers are thinking, "Wow, what is she doing right to have such an even-tempered, agreeable child?" But in my own dark moments, I wonder why my child *is* so robotic, so mechanical. Why she never seems to have a bad day. What does it all mean?

Even when it comes time to leave the park, I simply say, "Julia, it's time to go," and she pops herself in the stroller. I see other mothers spend twenty minutes negotiating with their child, and usually they must resort to a sugary treat to close the deal.

Today, like at every playdate, the broken and interrupted conversation revolves around parenting. Milestones. Diets. Sleeping schedules. The latest equipment. Extracurricular activities. Anxiety over nursery school admissions. Our group is spread on the grass. The children are feasting on Pirate's Booty and Cheerios, plunging their little hands into plastic containers some of the mothers have brought. Julia, in a rare moment, is on the blanket, sitting with her feet sticking out in front of her, chomping on what I assume are the snacks. But someone yells out, "Oh my God, she's choking!" I look up and her face is crimson. I grab her and pry open her mouth. There are blades of grass at the back of her throat. I put my fingers in her mouth and pull them out one at a time. She sputters and coughs.

"Here," someone said. "Give her water."

Julia takes the sippy cup and gulps hard. She looks up at the crowd of faces and then takes a few more sips of water. I hear someone say, "She's brave."

I assume she said that because Julia never cried during or after the scare.

"She's okay," someone else says.

"You okay, Julia?" another mother asks.

I hear a voice in my mind saying, *Go pick her up and embrace her.* But I don't because I know she's fine. I know in a moment she'll get back on her feet and start running around. I know that if I try to coddle her, she'll reject me in front of the crowd. I survey the faces of the other mothers, feeling judged, though there's a good chance that nobody will give this incident a second thought except me.

∞∞∞

"Make sure you keep those chips away from her," I bark, abruptly pulling the bowl away from Julia. The three of us are sitting at an outdoor table at a Mexican restaurant. It's a beautiful early summer evening, but I'm still shaken from today's incident.

"What's the matter?" Ricky says

I tell him how Julia was eating grass, but I hadn't noticed until a playgroup mother pointed it out and how I got to her in time, but still. . . . As usual, he reacts calmly, saying children get up to mischief.

"I know, but I think other mothers and their children are so in tune with each other. I'm just afraid one day something will happen, and it will be too late for me to come to her aid."

For once, Ricky does not gloss over my concerns with his eternal optimism. Instead, he grows quiet, contemplative.

∞∞∞

It's hot today, and I wish I was at the beach, sitting on a lounge chair, reading a book, alone and not at Riverside Park standing at the edge of a sandbox-turned-urban swimming pool. Julia is always the first child in, and she romps and splashes with gusto. She likes to squash her bottom right against the nozzles of the sprinkler. Most children approach the fountains tentatively. From the corner of my eye, I notice Vera tugging a pail from another child. Nancy slices through the shin-deep water like a motorboat to quell the mayhem. They're at a distance so I can't hear the words, but I can see Nancy trying to reason with Vera to give the pail back to the boy and Vera is thrashing and flailing.

I watch the scene and wonder if Julia would be territorial and possessive if I were more like Nancy. If I had worn her on my back or in a

Snugli when she was younger, if I fussed over her constantly, if we slept in a family bed, would Julia be more prone to jealousy, rage, moodiness? Does her lack of these emotions signal a problem?

∞∞∞

"Oh good, you're early," I say to Jen. "The locker room's upstairs."

Jen and I are taking a mommy-and-me swim class with Jason and Julia. In the locker room, I notice how Jen leaves Jason on the bench lying down, and she glides over to the locker to take out his swim trunks and a diaper. I watch this tableau in disbelief. She trusts him to remain on the bench until she returns, and he does. I picture mother ducks and their chicks and the natural order of things. I feel envy because it is never like that with Julia and me.

When in the pool, the water exercises force Julia to rely on me, which is good. She instinctively realizes she needs me to keep her safe and afloat, and she holds on and lets me guide her through the swimming exercises.

Back in the dressing room, we pull the wet suits off our toddlers and towel-dry them. Jason is drowsy; he's content to sit in his stroller and peck Cheerios. Julia is tooling around, heading for the toilet stall. Still dripping in my wet suit, I chase her.

∞∞∞

The first whiffs of fall are upon us. The air is crisper, the sky is bluer. The streets are busy again with postsummer seriousness. Riverside Park is not as crowded. My playgroup has been meeting a little less frequently. I'm relieved, because even though it provided structure and filled time, being around this group of nice mothers, a group I built, has been causing me pain and ambivalence. The more time I spend with them, the lonelier I become. The version of motherhood I witness contradicts everything I experience. I'm in some parallel universe feeling alienated, even angry. Last night Ricky asked me if I was still going to playgroup. I told him I was losing interest. He said he understood, but I didn't know if he really could.

Thirteen

It is 9:00 PM on Thursday, November 27. It is Thanksgiving Day, or at least it was when we left New York. We've come to London to spend four days with Leah and Brian and their two children, Maddy and Josh. At first it seemed sacrilegious when Ricky suggested Thanksgiving away from home and family, but I thought about it and it made sense. I'm barely speaking with my parents. They have not formed a bond with Julia. The same can be said about Ricky's family. So here we are, on a whim, at Heathrow Airport.

"There he is," I yell, squinting to see the name on the placard.

We hasten our step. Ricky is holding Julia in one arm and pulling our luggage with the other. I'm carrying lighter bags and clutching Julia's jacket. Her eyes are big round saucers, drinking in the commotion of humanity. I wave at the skinny man in the ill-fitting suit and floppy driver's cap.

"Hi, we're the Tannenbaums. Leah sent you, yes?"

"That's right," he says. "Can I give you a hand with your baggage, sir?" he asks, bending down before Ricky has a chance to answer.

He lifts the small suitcase with a grunt and says, "Wait o'er 'ere, love. I'll bring the car around."

Leah and I met when I lived in London from 1981 through 1987. Even now with an ocean between us, I think of her as the friend who understands me best.

Leah is waiting outside in a misty drizzle when we drive up along the shiny curb next to her house. Her blonde hair is blonder, cropped. She's wrapped in a gray wool cape, hunched slightly forward to shield the damp. She walks to the driver's window and leans in.

"Go ahead and put that on my account."

She straightens up and hugs Ricky as he exits the car.

"You've made it," she says, air kissing.

"Good to see you."

She pokes her head into the car.

"Hello, gorgeous," she says to me.

I want to hug her, but I've got Julia on my lap.

"Shall I take her from you?" she asks.

"Please do."

Julia hasn't slept since we left New York ten hours ago. She could not settle down on the plane. Up and down she went in her seat, manically playing I spy with the people in the row behind us.

Leah tugs Julia sideways from my lap. She holds her with one arm, like a Frenchman clasping a baguette, and then extends her other hand to fish me out of the car.

"Out you git, old girl," she says. We hug.

We walk through a gate inside a high stone wall and snake through a warren of rooms. Ricky tramps behind like an agreeable mule.

"Brian's back tomorrow night," Leah says. "The kids are already asleep. Why don't you settle in and we'll have a nosh. Dirty diapers go there. I've left some things in the fridge. Yogurts and such. Let me know if you need anything else."

"Let me change Julia," Ricky says, while she wriggles fiercely to get out of his arms. "I'll get her in pajamas. Maybe she'll go down after that."

"God, I hope so," I say.

I flop onto a bed with a fluffy white down comforter and curl into a fetal position. My lids are heavy, and my throat is dry from the stale plane air. I faintly hear Ricky puttering about with Julia. I know how lucky I am to have a husband who is so involved in raising our child, though sometimes I wonder if he's like that because I fall short.

I'm startled when Ricky nudges me.

"Do you want me to let you sleep?" he says softly.

"No, no, sorry, I'll get up. Leah's waiting for us. How long was I sleeping?"

"About twenty minutes. Julia's down in the crib. Went to sleep right away."

The blue sky is rinsed with streaky white clouds, nice for a London morning in November. Leah's house is a beehive of activity. Maddy, Leah's six-year-old, watches television. Josh, a cherubic boy with coiled blond curls trailing to his bare shoulders, zips around the living room in his diaper on a plastic truck, making *vroom vroom* noises. Ricky feeds Julia in a high chair at the dining room table. Leah gives instructions to a tanned young women who's nodding dutifully. The table is filled with juice, jam, breads, muesli, and empty teacups.

"Hello, sleeping beauty. Help yourself," Leah says. "Maddy, you have to eat before school."

"I don't want to," she hisses.

"I know, darling, but you must. Come have a piece of toast. Make Mummy happy."

"I don't want to," she whines louder.

"Tina, this is Katya," Leah says. "She's our nanny."

Katya holds out a hand to shake mine.

"Lovely to meet you," she says.

"And you," I say.

"I'm taking Maddy to school in twenty minutes. We'll leave for Kenwood around 11:00 AM."

∞∞∞

The morning chill is refreshing. North London splays before us from Kenwood, a historic hillside estate with a grand house and manicured grounds. Ricky pushes Julia in a borrowed stroller, Leah pushes Josh, and I walk in the middle of my two favorite people. We cover all the familiar topics: my relationship with my parents, Leah's family, my work, the rock bands Brian manages, updates on people we both know.

We park Ricky at a table with the two strollers and the babies.

"Be right back. We'll get some sandwiches." Leah loops her arm through mine. We are alone for the first time. "How's motherhood?"

"Not exactly what I was expecting."

Leah nods in a way that tells me I don't have to say any more. I also know I can say what I think without feeling judged.

"You look tired, thin," she says. "Is Julia a bad sleeper?"

"No, not at all. It's not that. I'm just, I don't know, overwhelmed. I'm not, how can I say this, feeling the joy. Does that make sense? I mean, don't get me wrong, I love Julia and I realize how blessed we are, but I am exhausted and I have stomachaches all the time."

"Why don't you think about getting a part-time nanny, someone reliable, so you'll have separate time to work and you'll feel more present when you're with Julia?" she suggests. "I know how it is. It's very hard to plunge into motherhood after forty. I mean, come on, you had a whole life before, and then suddenly, it's hijacked."

"You're right. It has been a really difficult transition, but it's more than just how different things were before Julia got here. The whole experience feels, I don't know, like I'm not in my own skin. It feels like the most unnatural thing I've ever done, which is the last thing I expected to feel about motherhood, you know?"

"I think you need to balance things up. I know how hard you work, and you need to delineate your time. Think about it. I couldn't live without Katya. She's a lifesaver."

I nod but say nothing. I fantasize what a day might look like if I had a nanny like Katya, and it sends an exhilarating tingle up my spine. Then I see myself handing Julia off to a stranger and I feel guilty.

Since becoming a mother, I have been caught in a revolving-door conversation with myself. Would everything be different if Julia had been a birth child? Of course it would. Would I have had a nanny lined up from the start, knowing I had to work? Probably. The idea of bonding with my child would have been a given or at least a strong assumption. Do I owe it to Julia to be her full-time caretaker? Do I owe her this because of what she's lost? I'm in a surreal corn maze with no sense of direction.

We carry sandwiches back to the table. I pull out a yogurt for Julia, and she gobbles it down. I cut strawberries and hand her tiny pieces.

Leah hovers over Josh waving a piece of cheese. The baby thrashes, volleying his pinched-up face from side to side, spitting.

"C'mon Joshy," Leah says. "C'mon, be a good boy."

"Does he want a yogurt?" Ricky says. "We have an extra in the bag."

"No," Leah says, furrowing her brow. "It's not that. He won't let me feed him. He wants Katya. He thinks she's his mother."

"What?" I say, surprised.

"It's true. He spends most of his time with her. We haven't formed a true bond yet."

Her words nearly knock me off my seat. I rest my sandwich.

"What? What did you just say?"

"I don't think we're really bonded yet. He doesn't seem to think I'm his mum."

Leah says this without any kind of pained expression on her face.

In that moment, I feel an odd feeling of satisfaction. One of the women I admire most in the world has not bonded with her baby, and she's not drowning in despair. She simply accepts that her eleven-month-old son, at least for now, is more attached to his nanny, but that over time, he'll love her. Her confidence is not in shambles. She's not beating herself up.

Leah makes one more attempt to feed the baby.

"Okay, Josh, suit yourself," Leah says, taking the food away from the baby and putting it back in her large bag.

The next three days, Ricky and I are treated to a whirlwind of pleasure: a film screening, theater, restaurants. Katya minds the three children.

On Sunday morning I squeeze Leah tightly, wishing we could stay longer.

"Thanks so much for everything."

"You'd better go. You might hit traffic on the M4."

Ricky and Julia are in the backseat. I slide in. Ricky hands me a tissue.

"It was a good trip," he says.

On the plane, I take out my diary and jot notes.

I write, "Hire full-time nanny," and I run a circle around the phrase three times.

Julia is sitting in the seat between Ricky and me. I lean over her and show Ricky the notation.

I search his eyes for approval.

Ricky reads the words and nods.

"Yes?" I say.

"Absolutely."

Fourteen

"I almost forgot," Anna says, slipping back into the apartment. "I made a set of these for you." She fishes for an envelope in her bulging faux leather bag and hands it to me with a beam of pride splashed across her young, fresh face. Inside is a batch of photos from the mommy-and-me ballet class Anna takes Julia to. I shuffle slowly through the stack, gazing at the images of tiny, tippy-toed ballerinas twirling, spinning, leaping in their pink bodysuits, tutus, and soft slippers. I see a little girl I don't know in these pictures. Julia participating in a group. She's part of something. One of. That's how it seems, anyway. She's not off in a corner or outside the circle. I draw one of the pictures closer to my eyes. Julia sits snugly against Anna looking relaxed. Anna has tied back her thin blonde strands with a pink ribbon. With Anna's blonde hair, blue eyes, and broad Polish face, she and Julia look more like mother and child than Julia and I do. I teeter on that thin line between horror and delight. The thought of Julia being in sync with another woman is heartening, even though that woman is not me.

"These are wonderful," I say, rearranging my taut face into a smile. "Thank you so much."

I hug her briefly.

"I'm glad you like them," she says, gingerly reopening the front door. "I better go. See you tomorrow."

Her footsteps fade as she walks to the elevator. I reopen the door quickly and call out her name, but it's too late. The elevator doors groan shut.

"Never mind," I say to myself. "Another time."

I wanted to ask Anna what it's like when she's with Julia. How *she* feels. Is it satisfying? Has she enjoyed being her nanny these past three months? When Anna came for the interview in late December, she glowed when she talked about two children she had taken care of for three years. She carried a picture of them. "These are my children," she had said, showing me the frayed photograph she kept in her wallet. Ricky thought it was slick salesmanship. I believed it was genuine love. When I called the mother of those children as a reference before hiring Anna, the woman gushed about Anna's dedication to her babies.

∞∞∞

Having Anna take care of Julia five days a week from nine to five while I work has released me from a suffocating inert existence. I can eat without constriction in my throat. I can go to the bathroom without straining. I can think. I had no idea caring for a baby all day long would leave me unable to care for myself, but it did. I wasn't able to coalesce with my child, to find a rhythm where neither of us was sacrificed. Constant preoccupation with her needs and mine wiped out moments that should have filled me, her, us, with joy. Ultimately I felt like an interloper in the mommy-and-me group I founded, and we stopped going. Never have I failed at anything so spectacularly.

∞∞∞

Anna is reliable, cheerful, and tender with Julia. She arrives every morning on time, carefully coiffed, a vision of loveliness. No matter how cold it is outside, she doesn't complain. She has found ways for her and Julia to fill long days outside the apartment so I can work. In addition to mommy-and-me classes, she does what I used to do: she strolls the avenues, ducking into Barnes & Noble and other shops to pass the time.

She also has nanny friends with young charges. She tells me they congregate in apartments where the babies play. I've gone from being completely frightened of having a stranger handle Julia to being ecstatically happy to have regained some of my freedom. When I spoke to Leah the other day, she said, "You did the right thing. There's no shame in having help." The first few weeks were a little nerve-racking. I'd check in with Anna every few hours on her cell, but I quickly felt I could trust her. Now I don't talk to her until she brings Julia back at the end of the day.

I imagine a conversation in which I look into Anna's blue eyes and ask her: *Do you love her? Does she love you? Do you love her the way you loved the two children you used to care for?* I need to know this, because I want to know if Julia can attach.

Anna is stoic, professional, and practical, and if she's having issues with Julia, she doesn't let on. But I have noticed that when she arrives in the morning, Julia doesn't run and greet her. At the same time Julia doesn't put up a fuss when Anna puts on her jacket and hat and wheels her out of the apartment. She shows no distress at leaving me. At day's end, Julia tumbles into the apartment. She's not affectionate or clingy with Anna. Did Anna need to hold Julia tight when someone snapped that loving photo? When Anna calls out to Julia and says "good-bye," Julia doesn't respond. She doesn't even look up.

I'm afraid that asking Anna these questions would cause her cheeks to puff up, her face to redden. *Of course I do*, she'd say, emphasizing each word with staccato crispness. I don't want to put her on the spot. I don't want her to tell me she loves Julia to protect her job. Or to protect me.

I run through the photos one more time. In one Julia is sitting on the wooden floor, her chubby legs and arms outstretched. She looks like a porcelain figure. Her dark eyes are bottomless. She seems lost in thought. She is a puzzle.

OOOOOO

I feel a warm kiss on the back of my neck as I make eggs in the kitchen.

"Happy Valentine's Day," Ricky coos.

"I thought I'd let you sleep late. Want eggs?"

"I needed the sleep," he says, pouring himself a cup of tea. "She's eaten?" he asks, gazing over at Julia, who is in her room, fifteen feet from the dining room table, toppling anything that stands vertically.

"Yep. Eggs?"

"Sure, eggs would be dandy. What do you want to do today?"

"Do you know what today is?"

Ricky looks perplexed.

"It's . . . " he looks over at the calendar. "It's Valentine's Day. I knew that. Did you want flowers?"

"No, not Valentine's Day, I mean yes, it's Valentine's Day, but why is this day special?"

Ricky's eyes narrow. He's beseeching me to tell him.

"It is exactly one year since we became Julia's parents. A year ago today we woke up in the Moscow Marriott with a baby in a laundry basket in our hotel room."

"Hard to believe. Mmm. Those eggs look good."

"Yeah, it's a funny thing, to associate her with Valentine's Day, no?"

"Better than all that forced flowers and chocolate stuff. She's our little Valentine."

I gaze at Ricky's sweet face. I often wonder what a biological child of ours would have looked like. I see her. A girl with high cheekbones, chestnut brown hair, and the green eyes we both have.

For a change, the apartment feels calm and peaceful. It's cold outside, and there's nowhere we have to be. I look at Julia, who is now climbing on and off the couch, and wonder if there will ever be a day when I temporarily forget that she is not my flesh and blood. Today, a year behind us, carries weight. It puts a marker in time. It's like an anniversary and birth rolled into one. We've been together for a year, but that day, to me, felt like her "birth." I drift back to last June 28, her first birthday, and recall how sad I was because I hardly felt anything except some vague pang of guilt for having become this child's mother. I thought about the young Russian girl who gave birth in the grim gunmetal gray hospital Olga showed us. Did she hold her? Did she cry when she handed her back to a nurse for the last time? Does she think about her long-lost baby on June 28, and does she regret her choices?

It's funny—we chose an international adoption because we wanted it to be clean and final and without interference. But sometimes I wish I could just steal a few secret moments to ask her questions that dog me.

∞∞∞

Three days later I arrive at Dr. Traister's office. I gave Anna the morning off so I could take Julia for her third well-visit. So far the doctor's been pleased with her progress. Dr. Michael Traister specializes in treating foreign-adopted children. He recommends a second round of vaccines when they come home because he doesn't trust the ones they've received in Russia. He knows to look for low muscle tone and aberrant neurological symptoms that might have gone undetected. He knows children with fetal alcohol syndrome don't always show signs of mental disorder right away. He's been very enthusiastic about Julia's progress. She walked at a year, started forming words a month later, is solid and strong.

"How's her eating?" he says, glancing over his bifocals to read her chart.

"She's on a fully organic, whole-foods, non-meat diet," I say.

"Meaning?"

"Fruits, veggies, grains, eggs, lots of yogurt, everything organic. But no cow's milk."

"Okay, that's good. She's actually in the 95th percentile for her weight. But that's because she's small."

"Her birth mother isn't even five feet," I say.

"Right, I understand. I'm not too worried about her weight now, though it may be an issue later on. But she looks great. You're doing a good job."

Those words are as comforting as his assessment on Julia's progress.

Dr. Traister is one of the godsends that have come along with my entry into motherhood. When someone first recommended him, I thought he and I, who have practically the same last name—an unusual name—could be related. The doctor and I tried to find common ancestors as we are both from Brooklyn, but we couldn't make the link. While that might be so, I feel as though this wiry-haired, jeans-wearing, Gene Wilder look-alike, could well be kin. He's familiar. And best of all, he's relaxed and conservative in his approach to medicine. When I was a child, we made ritualistic pilgrimages to the pediatrician for every cough, sniffle, and ache. We were over-medicated. It was either that my mother was neurotically fearful about health or that she had a wicked crush on Dr. Kane. Over the years I've receded from the notion that doctors are gods and have replaced it with the idea that the human body is a machine that has the power to heal and regenerate. I steer clear of intervention unless it's truly necessary. I plan to raise Julia this way, and Dr. Traister, as I've said, is a godsend.

"Okay, you can dress her. Make an appointment in six months, and we'll talk about vaccines," he says.

"Great, thanks," I say, turning to pull Julia's sweater over her head. I hesitate. "Dr. Trais . . . "

"Yes," he says, poking his head around the reopened door.

"Sorry, I know you have another appointment, but I did have one more question."

"Sure, what is it?"

"How do I know if Julia is okay, you know, mentally?"

"What do you mean?"

"I don't know. It's just that, I can't explain this exactly, but sometimes, no, well, most of the time, it's like she's there but she's not there. She doesn't cling to me or look me in the eye or seem to enjoy being held. You know, she doesn't reach for my hand. I know it's not a hearing problem. It's more like, like there's a wall."

While I'm rambling, Dr. Traister is nodding.

"Am I making sense?"

"You could be describing something called Reactive Attachment Disorder."

"What?" I say, not entirely surprised by his answer.

"There's a syndrome in adopted children, particularly from Russia and Eastern Europe, called Reactive Attachment Disorder, where babies have trouble attaching to their adoptive parents. It's a complex condition, and it may be too early to diagnose this yet because Julia's only eighteen months old. But the gist of it is that babies who start life in orphanages haven't had the same bonding experiences as those who have been raised by birth mothers. As I said, it may be too early to know if this is the case with Julia, but if you want to make another appointment to come back and talk about this—or if you want I can suggest a child psychologist. Just see the nurse on your way out."

He smiles. "Don't worry. You have time."

My throat's gone dry. The exam room's bright lights sear into my brain. I was hoping Dr. Traister would say I was the one who was experiencing difficulty, ambivalence, maybe even postpartum depression. That it was me who needed "more time" to adjust to motherhood. I gaze down at the little blonde girl on the table and choke back tears.

"More time," I whisper. "We need a little more time." I lift her up and carry her to the waiting room. I slide her into the stroller. Before I pull open the heavy door, I glance back over my shoulder at the front desk. Dr. Traister's words protect me: *Don't worry. You have time.* I let the heavy door swing shut.

Fifteen

"Julia, wait, waaaait . . ." I scream, but it's pointless. "Goddamn it." She's barreling across a grassy mound toward an elaborate wooden labyrinth of layers to climb and explore. It has swinging bridges and watchtowers and secret passages and a sandbox. The village of New Paltz presents an impressive castellum compared to the bland iron relics on our playground at 97th in Riverside Park. She is barely in sight. Ricky has accelerated his gait to catch up with her. We want to encourage Julia to walk rather than push her in a stroller, but she's impossible to hold onto. She won't clutch a hand; she refuses to stay close. There is no duckling instinct. As soon as her little feet hit the ground, she takes off. Strangers may think it's cute—a little girl embracing her "terrible twos"—but Ricky and I know something is wrong. At this age, most children will stretch their wings to a point, but they retract when they instinctively know they've crossed an invisible line. Julia doesn't do this. She's deaf to our frightened pleas. Indifferent to our distress. She has none of her own when she separates from us. I have come to believe there is something intentional about this behavior because she does it every time. Although she is not intellectually calculating this maneuver, I think subconsciously she's trying to say, *See, I'm in control. You can't get near me.*

The other day she and I were at Barnes & Noble. I was trying to read to her, but as always she was disinterested and wandered away. I got up to follow her, expecting to find her ducking behind by the shelves—not hide-and-seek but the usual taunt. She wasn't there or seemingly anywhere within thirty feet. My heart started racing. I looked around and headed toward the center of the store. I gasped when I saw her teetering at the top of a steeply declining eighty-foot-long escalator that drops to the first floor. I wasn't sure what to do. If I called out her name it might propel her to take a fatal step forward, and if she did that, she'd certainly tumble to her death. As I neared the escalator, I saw other patrons closing in on her. The whole place seemed to freeze, and then in a surreal slo-mo moment, I snatched the back of her T-shirt and pulled her away from the precipice. She fell on her bottom and looked stunned, but she didn't cry. I grabbed her arm roughly and sat on the ground. The room spun. I was dizzy. I put my head in my hands. I thought I was going to pass out, but a few people gathered around me and asked me if I was all right, if I needed some water. I said I was okay. I felt embarrassed, though to these bystanders I probably looked like an action hero in a Hollywood movie. I suppressed the urge to cry until we got outside, and then I sobbed the whole way home while I wheeled her in her stroller.

∞∞∞

Ricky's out of sight but I hear him screaming, "Stop, Julia, stop!" Five minutes later I'm cresting the hill. I see the sun-flaming orange dot that is Julia's dress and the top of my heroic husband's head bopping and weaving as he spots her on the jungle gym. I often wonder, with horror, what it would be like to be a single parent with a child like Julia. I think about Jo, who traveled with us in Russia, a single mother of two internationally adopted children.

The playground is filled with what Ricky and I call *Chitty Chitty Bang Bang* children. Blond and shaggy, they look slightly wild and unshackled compared to their Upper West Side counterparts. It's probably just an illusion in this border-confined, hyperparenting universe, but these children look like little hippies in tie-dye from the local Groovy Blueberry and little Birkenstock-type sandals. Mom, who's fortysomething, keeps her gray hair natural. Dad's got a goatee and an earring.

Julia is in the sandbox, which is six feet from where I am sitting. She's commandeered some kid's pail and she's making sand pies. Ricky is dutifully attentive.

A woman sits next to me. She wipes her brow with the back of her hand and smiles at me.

"Is she yours?"

"Yes," I say, while I hear the voice inside my head that says, *Not really.*

"She's adorable.

"Thanks. We're visiting."

"Where are you from?"

"The city."

It is understood what city I'm referring to.

The playground patter begins, though it's not the usual chore because I'm interested in her story. She and her husband are Brooklyn transplants. They came to New Paltz, a hip college town two hours north of Manhattan, three years ago after the birth of their first baby. They have two now, and for a while her husband commuted to the city, but a year ago they started making and packaging granola. Now they are building a business that is thriving, thanks, in part, to the great support she's had from local vendors.

"Wow," I say, thinking how wholesome it all sounds. "Was it hard to leave Brooklyn? Do you miss it?"

"It was difficult at first; we were definitely scared," she said. "But it's been fantastic. This is a great town. We've made good friends. The kids are happy. Here, wait, let me write down my number. If you come up this way again, give me a call. And check out our granola. The bakery sells it."

I say good-bye and drift over to Ricky and Julia.

"How's she doing?" I ask.

"Great. She likes this place."

"So do I. I just met the nicest woman. Let's get some lunch. It's getting late."

ooooooo

We choose a busy bistro on Main Street. I lay the menu on the table.

"What?" I say. "Why are you looking at me that way?"

"What way? I'm not looking at you any way. What are you having? What is Julia having?"

"I'll have eggs. I'll get her yogurt and fruit."

Despite the fact that I've practically written in blood that I will never leave Manhattan's hallowed ground, Ricky knows I'm weakening. He's aware my love affair with Manhattan has dimmed since 9/11. I'm hankering for change, but I'm too scared to admit it to myself, let alone anyone else. So he bides his time, waiting, like the patient saint that he is, for me to let go.

ooooooo

For the past eight months, we've spent every weekend visiting suburbs and small towns up and down the Hudson Valley. We're not house-hunting, per se. I pretend we take these weekend excursions because I write a column for the *New York Post*'s real estate section about living in such towns. But the truth is—and Ricky knows this—I could easily gather this material online and by phone. Exploring this territory, however, is a safe way for me to look at the merchandise without purchasing. I'm window shopping. And Ricky, who is quietly tactical, has got me watching HGTV nonstop. It's a slow-drip intravenous drug.

With each road trip we wander through a town, popping into bakeries, visiting playgrounds, checking out stores. I take note if a town has a bookstore, health-food shop, and swimming pool—things that are important to me. I pick up the local newspaper. Lately I'll do an errand, such as go to the post office or buy glue at a hardware store. I'm getting beyond window shopping—I'm inside the dressing room trying towns on for size. Best find of all is the local bulletin board sheathed in fliers, ads, and requests in a coffee shop where I find out about a yoga class or a concert or a lost cat. It's like putting my ear up against someone's chest and listening to her heartbeat. Then we drive around and look at houses. Inevitably on some main road near town or on a hill on the outskirts I see an old farmhouse and I screech, "Wait, stop!" Ricky slows down and brings the car to a halt. I roll down the window and gawk, like a lovesick teen. I say something like, "That's a beautiful old house," or "Wouldn't it be great to have a covered porch like that?" And Ricky says, "Absolutely." Then he asks coyly, "Are you ready?" and he seemingly means am I ready to go back home now, but I get the double meaning of his question.

Mondays after our jaunts, I finish my story research by phone in interviews with city folks who, like the woman I met in the New Paltz playground, have relocated. Their personal anecdotes add a human touch to the column, which is filled with practical information. I only need fifteen minutes to extract a good quote, but I can't get off the phone. As soon as they start talking, I'm a fish on the end of a reel. I want to hear it all. How they finally made the decision to leave. How they chose this town, their house. What it's been like. Do they have regrets? These people are as happy to talk as I am to listen. One woman told me about standing at her kitchen window, watching her daughter swing on a rubber tire that hangs from an old oak tree in their front yard. Another man related how he sits on his deck after his commute back from the city. He said he loves to watch the deer munching on his shrubs at dusk. After each call, I'm lost in thought. If this were us, would things be different? Would Julia settle down? Would I enjoy motherhood? Would an old farmhouse surrounded by tall trees take away the hurt?

"Do you remember . . . " I shout, then pause to wait for the moaning fire engine to rumble past the outdoor cafe on Amsterdam Avenue where Ricky, Julia, and I are eating dinner. "Do you remember that lake house we rented a few years ago?"

"The one in Ellenville?"

"Yeah, John and Carroll's house."

"Sure. What about it?"

"Why don't we rent it again this summer? We can do a few weekends and maybe a two-week stretch in August."

"Sounds interesting. How would that work?"

"Well, the rental is very reasonable. I could work out six weekends."

"What about Julia? Where would she sleep?"

"There's the second bedroom on the ground floor."

"We'd need to get a crib in there."

"We could get one from IKEA and build it in the room."

"Call Carroll. See if it's possible."

Three years ago, Ricky and I rented John and Carroll's house for summer weekends. Being in the Catskills took me back to sleepaway camp. It had been two decades since I'd swum across a lake or laid back in the grass and stared at a starry sky. The snug two-story bungalow was basic, with loose wires, unpainted walls, and clattering appliances, but the view of the dappled lake from the large living room window and the silence at night were restorative.

The house is still available, and I book it. When I tell Ricky about the two-week stretch, he suggested having Anna come with us. I thought it was a brilliant idea.

By July we are spending weekends in the country. On Fridays, we load the car with food, toys, books, clothes, and our cat. Two hours later, with the sun sinking behind the brooding Catskill peaks, we take a left off Route 209 and turn onto a rough mountain road. Concrete and commotion is replaced with desolation and ruin. The ghostly path is lined with abandoned bungalow colonies and hollowed-out horse ranches from the long-lost days when the Catskill Mountains were a first-class tourist destination. Every other house is for sale. One family keeps a herd of goats. The Hotel Rainbow on the right, now a camp, is filled with wool-wearing Hasidim milling about the grounds. Finally we turn onto Camp Road to Carroll's house. My chest releases. There's more space in it. I'm like an asthmatic sucking an inhalant.

We walk down to the lake at dusk to watch the water lilies close, as though there were tiny invisible storekeepers pulling down iron gates. The peepers belch; a gaggle of geese look like a fleet of lawnmowers. Slowly, the silence takes over.

Mornings are fresh and pregnant with hope. I take Julia with me to pluck graceful fire lilies and gather them in bunches for a table bouquet. Later, Ricky squeezes Julia between his knees while we row across the lake in a canoe to a tiny sandy beach for a picnic. Lately I've returned to painting, a childhood passion. On canvasses, in sketchbooks, and on smooth rocks, I paint or draw a house, a village of houses, or a pastoral scene with many houses. I use dabs of color to put flowers in the window boxes, and I apply quick strokes to make a picket fence. I'm not ready to house-hunt, so I house-dream. I'm a child at play, insinuating myself into a fairy tale, lost in a world I can only get to through paint.

"That's a nice one," Ricky says, peering over my shoulder.

I've painted a row of stone French village houses strung together like pearls. On one I added an awning and a sign, "Julia's Cafe."

"When Julia has a real room one day, I'll hang them on the wall."

Ricky squeezes my shoulder.

"That will be wonderful," he says.

I squint at the clock in the bedroom. It's 6:00 AM. I hear Anna downstairs with Julia. Since we arrived ten days ago, Anna has been caring for Julia in the morning while Ricky and I sleep until 8:00 AM, a luxury we've not had in nearly eighteen months. My body's been trained to wake at six, so it's hard to drift back to sleep. It's easier when I hear the flimsy screen door creak closed because I know Anna has taken Julia outside in the stroller for a walk.

It's been strange to have Anna with us in the Catskills. It's no surprise she works diligently to keep Julia fed, clean, and occupied. She's given me and Ricky the freedom to take a few hours for ourselves, day and night. What does feel odd is watching Anna tend to Julia when we're in the house or car together. I see Anna works as hard as we do to corral Julia. Julia isn't any more inclined to listen to Anna than she does to us. Anna's steely determination wins the day, and she perseveres without complaining. She never looks defeated, though now I see how Julia can tire even a seemingly indefatigable twenty-five-year-old.

One night after Julia falls asleep, Anna and I are sitting on the couch watching *The Wizard of Oz.* During commercials, we chat about her family in Poland. Eventually the conversation turns to Julia, and she asks me to tell her more about Julia's adoption from Russia. When I hired Anna eight months ago, I'd mentioned Julia was adopted but said nothing more. I did a quick recap on the Siberian odyssey and told Anna how we spirited Julia out of the orphanage in the middle of the night and flew in another snowstorm until dawn. I knew I could keep her captivated, but I decided it was time. So I took a sharp turn.

"Adopting a child, is, well, it makes things different."

"What do you mean?" she asks.

"Julia's difficult, different. No?"

Not sure what to say, I put her at ease.

"Don't get me wrong. You do an awesome, awesome job with her, and Ricky and I are so happy to have you. But now I've had a chance to see you and Julia together, and I see some of the same strange things I experience when I'm with her."

"You mean . . ."

"I mean she's hard to manage. She doesn't listen. She never relaxes."

"That's for sure," Anna says tentatively.

"And it's hard to be peaceful with her, no?" I say.

"Well, she never, well, almost never, cries, and she's never in a bad mood, which is interesting," Anna says. "But it's true, she's never, em, what's the word? Cozy."

"Cozy? What do you mean?"

"It's like she has a wall around her," she says.

Finally someone else has said what I've been feeling. She's lifted the curse. It's not me. We watch the end of the movie.

"Good-night Anna," I say before climbing the spiral stairs to the loft bedroom. "Thanks for being honest with me."

Upstairs, I join Ricky in bed. He's reading. I nudge him.

"Did you hear what Anna said about Julia having a wall around her?"

"I did," he says.

"And?"

"It's true. It's very hard to get through to Julia."

"I thought you thought it was just me—that I was, you know, not cut out for this mothering stuff."

"I don't know why you say that."

"Because that's what I thought you thought."

Ricky pulls me toward him.

"Let's get some sleep."

Sixteen

An eggplant-purple sky looms in the distance. The terrain becomes more mountainous every ten miles. Traffic moves swiftly along the New York State Thruway. We allotted two hours of travel time to make the afternoon performance of *The Nutcracker* at the Bardavon Theater in Poughkeepsie.

"Tell me what I need to do when we get off the Thruway," Ricky says.

"Okay," I say, lowering the volume on *The Nutcracker* CD that's playing and reaching for the directions in my bag.

We veer off the Thruway and cross the Mid-Hudson Bridge. The river, wide and expansive up here in the Upper Hudson Valley, is roiling. We wind through downtrodden urban streets choked with abandoned buildings before turning onto Market Street, which is lit with Christmas tinsel. Poughkeepsie, an old industrial upstate city, has been in decline since the 1960s. The Bardavon is one of its gems, maybe its shiniest. We could have taken Julia to see *The Nutcracker* much closer to our apartment, but this is research. More research on what it's like to be a denizen of a region that retains many characteristics that inspired the Hudson River School of painters.

I do my best to squelch my mother's negative words, which coil through my mind like a poisonous snake: "Why are you taking Julia to see *The Nutcracker* in some dinky theater in, what's the name of that town anyway?" she had said a couple of days ago on the phone.

"As I've explained already, it costs four times more to go to Lincoln Center," I'd said defensively. "Besides, it's not a dinky theater. The Bardavon is a historic theater. It's an important venue in the Hudson Valley. And did you know that a couple of ballet dancers from the New York City Ballet company are in the performance?"

She wasn't listening.

"I don't know," she'd said, emitting her teakettle sigh. "When you and your sister were young, we took you to Lincoln Center. There's nothing like Lincoln Center."

"Okay. Next year you can take Julia to Lincoln Center," I had said, knowing that will never happen because over the last two years my mother has not taken a genuine interest in being Julia's grandmother, and my relationship with her continues to grow more stormy.

A man in a neon orange vest is waving us into a parking lot across the street. Julia wakes, startled from a nap, but the buzz of parking, gathering our belongings, and families walking past our car heading toward the theater distracts her. She recovers this time without crying. Ricky and I each hold one of her outstretched mitten-clad hands as we walk toward the flashing Art Deco marquee and through the polished wood and glass doors. The lobby crackles with excitement. Tea and sugar cookies are being served. Mothers fuss over their tiny blonde girls in green or red velvet dresses, white tights, and Mary Janes. One mother spits on her hand and smooths the flyaway hairs in her little girl's braids. Another is buying her daughter a program. The child is whining. She wants popcorn.

We whisk past the crowd, enter the theater, and take our seats. Above us is a recessed ceiling dome lit in soft electric blue. A current of excitement electrifies the room. Every adult in the theater has probably seen *The Nutcracker* one or countless times, but now it's our turn to pass along this gift. The opening scene around the Christmas tree is as idyllic on this stage as it would be on any other. The music is recorded, not live, but it works. I peer at Julia, who is seated next to me, and my stomach knots. She's already shifting restlessly in her chair.

"You are going to see a beautiful ballet," I tell her, putting my hands up over my head to look like a ballerina. I'm hoping she'll find some connection between what's happening on the stage and what she does in the ballet class Anna brings her to. But I don't see an eager child with an open expression. I see a child who's not here with us, who is trapped inside her mind. A child who is ready to sabotage the possibility of something pleasant. As soon as the curtain rises, she is on and off the chair, snapping it back each time with a wallop. I glance over my shoulder and apologize to the patron behind us. It's as though she doesn't even know she's *in* a theater or that what's going on up on stage is meant to be watched. The next time she's on the chair I press her leg to keep her still, but it's useless. She wriggles more forcefully and jumps off the chair. I pull her back and point to the ballerinas, saying, "Look, look," but she won't. Ricky, who's sitting on my other side, sees I'm struggling. He reaches over me and pulls Julia on his lap. He tries to direct her attention to the stage, but she's climbing him like a pea plant twisting up a vine. I notice there are plenty of two-and-a-half-year-olds like Julia sitting calmly, watching with awe. A memory pops to mind. When she was around nine months, someone, and I can't remember who, had said, "Think of her as a newborn infant trapped in a nine-month-old's body." What she meant was that Julia's emotional life wasn't synchronized with her chronological age. She needed to catch up because she'd never been given what she craved as a newborn, or so went the theory. It's confusing, because Julia crawled, walked, talked, and even potty trained early and without much effort. Maybe the two forms of development—physical and emotional—are not always connected.

I should be tolerant and able to feel her pain. That I'm not makes me feel like a brute. I want my daughter to love sugar plum fairies in a deep purple forest.

By the time the performance ends, Julia has passed out on Ricky's shoulder. The battle to resist and fight finally exhausted her. Ricky carries her as we walk up the aisle.

"Hungry," she says, rubbing her eyes as she wakes.

"We're going to eat," Ricky tells her.

"Sorry," I say to Ricky. "I know that was difficult."

"It's not a big deal. Maybe she's just not ready for this kind of thing yet."

"Maybe. Did you see how many little girls her age were in the audience sitting quietly or at least attentively?" I whisper in his ear.

"I know, but it's not a big deal."

I'm silent. Processing sadness. I laugh to myself imagining Julia at Lincoln Center with my mother, not watching *The Nutcracker*, a performance that is twice as long as today's.

The car is icy.

"Cold up here," I say, my lips chattering.

Ricky fiddles with the heater buttons.

Julia is babbling loudly. In a low hush I say, "I know she couldn't sit still and it wasn't easy for you—or me. But you know, I don't think it was a total waste of time. Music finds its way into the soul."

"Don't worry so much."

"I can't help it," I say, choking back tears.

We leave the theater parking lot. Light snowflakes drizzle on us. Not much light remains in the flat sky.

"It's beautiful out here. Let's get a bite in New Paltz before we head back to the city."

∞∞∞

It is Martin Luther King Jr. Day and it's biting but blue. Julia is home with Anna. For months, we've been looking at houses. An offer we made on a New Paltz house fell through. Last week, we saw a tiny village house in Nyack, a pretty Victorian village on the western banks of the Hudson River. The house wasn't right, but the hilly community seemed appealing. Nancy, the broker at the open house, handed me her card and mouthed "call me." I called the next day, and we spoke for quite a while. I reminisced about the wonderful summer we'd had in the Catskills and how much I loved living on the lake, surrounded by tall trees and wildlife. So today, Ricky, Nancy, and I are trudging through thigh-high snow along an unplowed path leading to the side door of an old farmhouse perched on a mountain precipice. To our left is an enormous expanse of snow-covered woods. Finally, we step onto a creaky porch and shake loose the snow. Nancy struggles with the lock. Eventually it gives, and she uses her boot to push open the wooden door. The entryway is filled with cobwebs. The owner has relocated to Pennsylvania; no one's lived here for years. It looks more like decades. It's more a ruin than it is a house. Like a child in a haunted house, I'm thrilled. We pass into a large open space that passes for a kitchen and dining area but is a graveyard of sad appliances. I twist on the water tap, which emits brown liquid. We turn right into the next "room," which has an enormous burn from an old iron stove tattooed on its tilting floor. By the time we walk through the front hall and make another right, we are standing in the living room in front of a masculine brick hearth.

"You're not interested in seeing the upstairs, are you?" Nancy says, assuring us there are other houses to see.

"No," I say, "I would like to see upstairs."

Up the narrow, wood-paneled stairway there is one bedroom on either side of the house and a bathroom in between. The bedrooms are large, though the ceiling couldn't be more than six-and-a-half feet high. I've seen outhouses that rival this bathroom, though I do notice an old iron claw-foot tub.

"Okay, then," Nancy says in her chipper real-estate voice. "Shall we move on?"

We come down the steps and walk toward the side door.

"Can I have another minute?" I say.

Nancy looks perplexed, but she and Ricky go outside onto the porch.

I sweep by the wall of windows in the kitchen-dining area. Right outside the windows is a pair of deer traipsing across the snow, working as hard as we did earlier to navigate deep snow drifts. Their beauty hypnotizes me. I want to sit in front of that large hearth in the living room with a pot of cocoa.

"Do you believe in spells?" I say.

"Sorry," Nancy says. "We can move on."

"Um, okay. But I'm not discounting this house."

"It's a money pit. Let's keep looking."

She pulls the door a couple of times before it shuts properly.

Nancy shows us a handful of houses that day. Riding back to the city, I ask Ricky what he thinks about the old farmhouse.

"I can see why you like it," he says. "It has good bones. And really nice light."

"Yeah, but maybe Nancy's right. The house needs a total rehab."

I think back on the fifty or so houses we have seen in the last two months. This house felt different. That woozy way your heart and stomach react when you fall in love. I realize rationally the house is a pile of work, which is ironic because thus far I've rejected houses that needed only a coat of paint or new tiling. But something tugs at me. Something intangible. It's a vexing cocktail, taking a sad, ghostly thing and rescuing it. It's not about what's there but what's possible. Does this house attract me because it's another chance to rescue that which needs to be saved?

"You're going to think I've gone mad, but I think we should make an offer on the house," I say, as we turn onto West End Avenue.

"I don't think you're mad. I understand love is irrational. Make an offer. See what happens."

The next day I call Nancy and tell her to make an offer.

"The owner will never accept that," she says.

"I think she will," I say. "I'm not moving on the offer. That's my offer."

Fifteen minutes later, Nancy calls to tell me the offer is accepted.

I am thrown back to the day the social worker from the adoption agency called and said, "We have a baby for you."

It felt right and wrong, exciting but terrifying, crazy but sane.

Seventeen

"Julia, get off the bookcase. You're going to hurt yourself."

I spring from my desk chair and yank her off the bookshelves. I redirect her toward her bedroom, where she tosses herself on and off her "little girl" bed wildly.

"C'mon, let's get ready. Today's a big day. You start nursery school. Isn't that exciting?"

I pull on her blue corduroy pants and a pink long-sleeved shirt. It's hard to dress her because she isn't pliable or accommodating.

"Okay, that looks nice. Julia, get me your brush. It's over there, on the floor. Under Elmo."

She stares at me blankly.

"Go on, the brush," I say, making hair-brushing strokes on my own hair. "Bring it to me."

I know she hears me. I know she understands the words. She has what I call the "serial killer look" on her face. It's an expression that says, *I'm trifling with you and I'm enjoying it.* There's a wicked glint in her eye. A subtle grin. The more distressed I get, the more pleased with herself she seems to be.

What is this about? Why is a two-and-a-half-year-old so vested in such oppositional behavior? I'd expect it from an angry adolescent who hates the world or her mother.

I love the movie *Gaslight* where Charles Boyer attempts to make his wife, Ingrid Bergman believe she is going mad. Bergman slowly falls for her husband's deceptive plot because she closes herself off from the external world and there is nobody to remind her she's perfectly sane until the end. Being Julia's mother feels like this. To the world beyond this apartment, Julia is a charming, outgoing, engaging, energetic (these are some of the common adjectives I hear) little girl. She turns it on. She works the room. I'm often haunted by the first time she was put in my arms. She flashed a smile that I had, back then, described as "flirtatious."

"Okay," I say. "Don't brush your hair."

I walk out of her room. I'm disappointed. She knows it.

Even if a young child were playing a psychological tug-of-war over getting a brush, if in fact the object of the child's intention were the brush, the exiting of the mother might cause the child remorse shortly after. Not Julia. She is singing.

I glance at a letter lying open on my desk. It says parents should come forty-five minutes early the first day of nursery school because children have a tough time adjusting. I snort. I know there will be no tears or tantrums. Julia has never made a fuss, not once. The lack of drama is what makes it dramatic. But I've witnessed gory separation scenes, and I often count myself lucky that it isn't me in the situation. A child is inconsolable. The mother is at her wits' end. A child looks like she is going to vomit. So does the mother.

I'm walking with Julia up West End Avenue to the Purple Circle. I clench her hand tightly, but she's straining to get loose. I pull her back because the streets are slippery with wet snow. "Are you ready for nursery school?" I ask her. She doesn't look up. I think about Anna, and already I miss the reliable routine we had established over the past fifteen months. But everything is changing. We are buying a house in the Hudson Valley. We have sold our apartment. By July, we will leave the city and live in the Ellenville lake house while our new house undergoes a monster renovation. I cried when I told Anna the news. Her eyes moistened too. I begged her to stay on for evenings and weekends. It's inevitable she will fade from our lives. I explained to her we thought Julia needed a school setting. She understood, but she was hurt.

We enter the large brick synagogue on West 100th Street and ride the elevator to the fifth floor. An overweight woman holding a clipboard directs us toward a room beside a classroom. Down a long hallway beyond a bathroom and a wall of cubbies is a tight sitting area with couches and bookshelves. I take a seat, but Julia is buzzing about, grabbing picture book after picture book scattered on the table and in boxes. A woman asks if I'm Julia's mother and extends her open hand. "Welcome to the Purple Circle," she says. I feel like I'm a guest on a talk show. "You can put Julia's jacket and lunch box in this cubby." Then she turns to say "Hi Julia! I'm Janet. How are *you* today?"

Julia runs to Janet and gives her a loose hug.

"I know all the letters of the alphabet," she says.

"*Wow,*" says Janet. "That's *wonderful.*"

It's public Julia. Eager to please. She reminds me of a starlet who can turn on charm, flash a smile, and dazzle with her lashes but just as easily morph into a brooding handful when she's offstage.

Janet asks Julia if she'd like to visit the classroom.

Julia sticks out her hand to be held.

Janet looks at me, checking to see if I want to come too.

I gesture for her to take Julia to the adjoining room without me.

Two minutes later, Janet returns on her own.

"That is some independent child," she says.

"Yes," I nod, realizing I live in *The Twilight Zone.*

"Well," Janet says, clapping her hands together.

Before she can finish, I stand up.

"I think it's okay for me to leave, yes? Her dad will pick her up at 6:00 PM."

"Don't worry. She'll be fine," she says.

She doesn't have to tell me that. Julia will be fine. She will not miss me. I won't miss her either.

On the way out, I hear a child wailing. As I walk back toward the elevator, I see a mother dressed in a business suit clutching her lanky, hysterical son who is blubbering so hard he's hyperventilating. In between sobs he says, "No, Mommy! Don't go! Don't leave me!" The mother looks pained.

I skip past them and step onto the elevator.

I remember how hard it used to be to leave my mother's side when I went to sleepaway camp and then to college. I had no problem integrating in social situations, but I ached for my mother's assurances that everything would be all right. Right up through my divorce, my mother's voice was a constant in my day. I never felt completely separated from her, the way I do now.

The fresh morning tingles. I head back to the apartment and prepare for a day of juggling responsibilities for our house purchase, our apartment sale, and our temporary rental in Ellenville. There is so much to be done.

A routine forms. Every morning I ride up the elevator with Julia. When the doors open she tears away from me like a Tasmanian Devil and disappears into the classroom. When I call out good-bye, she doesn't wave. I ask the teachers how she is doing. They tell me she is a delight. She knows everyone's name, and she's extremely generous. Every evening Ricky walks through the door with her at 6:15 PM. He doesn't understand why she's so filthy. The smell of stale yogurt permeates her shirt. Her fingers and face are sooty with grime—she looks like an urchin.

"Why can't they take her to the bathroom and clean her up?" he asks, annoyed.

"I've mentioned it," I say. "They tell me she likes to explore on her knees."

"They've got no interest in her," he says.

"It's true," I say. "It's a warehouse. They tell you what you want to hear. Their mission is to get through the day."

Ricky sighs, and the conversation changes to real estate.

The last thing left to do is get our two cats into their carriers. Nothing remains in the apartment except scuffed walls, worn wooden floors, and strewn wrapping materials the movers left behind. Both of our cars are packed and waiting to be driven from the gate of this old life. Today we are heading for the Ellenville lake house where we will live for three and a half months. I have devised a grand plan. We will commute nearly two hours to Nyack each day. Julia will start a new nursery school. I have rented an office for work, and I'll be managing the house renovation. Ricky will travel to the city and the surrounds for business. At the end of each day, we'll head back to the mountains. On weekends, we will remain upstate but work on outfitting the house. I've given the contractor a Halloween deadline.

Ricky comes into the apartment and lifts a cat carrier in each hand.

"Where's Julia?" I say.

"Julia, Julia," Ricky bellows. Then I hear her voice in the hallway.

"Are you ready?" Ricky asks me.

"I need a minute. I'll meet you downstairs. I'm going to follow you in the car. We're taking the Palisades, right?"

He nods and disappears.

I go back into the bedroom. I want the memories, good and bad, to soak into my skin. It's been seven years since I moved in, single with my dog, broken but hopeful, determined to teach myself to be strong and independent. So much has happened since that March day. I unpacked every box, filled every bookshelf, and hung every picture before I went to sleep that night.

I glance at the tiny bathroom, thinking how impossible it was to kneel by the tub and bathe Julia because most of the tub was lined up against the toilet. I walk slowly through the living room recalling how when I first bought the apartment and it was still empty, I'd come in the evening and sit in the middle of the floor and sketch plans for my furniture layout. How over the years so much more furniture was squeezed in to accommodate me plus husband plus child. I walk into Julia's room, which was really only ever a glorified foyer and not the nursery a mom takes pride in, but Julia put her stamp on it. I notice a torn cover of an old picture book sticking out under the closet door. I take one final lap around the kitchen and stand at the window where I've spent my treasure working and worrying and making a spectacular life unfold. I toss a set of keys on the counter and break down sobbing. I pull tight the heavy door for the last time. Then I jiggle the taut door handle. The past is behind me.

∞∞∞

By late summer, our new house has been stripped to the studs, every inch of obsolete infrastructure has been pulled out, and floors have been ripped up. There is a Dumpster on the property filled with old wood and a Porta-Potty for the crew working day and night. One day I'm at my temporary office working. Ricky calls.

"Listen, I think you might get upset when you get to the house," he says. "They've taken off the roof. The house looks, I don't know, vulnerable. I just wanted to warn you."

I push aside my work and grab my car keys. I'm bracing myself for the shock. I swing into the driveway and clatter down the sloping path. I can see the gaping opening from the top of the driveway. Ricky is talking to the foreman. I stop midway and put my hands over my face. Ricky sprints over to me. Tears are streaming down my face.

"I warned you," he says. "It will be okay."

"No, no, you don't understand," I say. "This is the most beautiful thing I have ever seen. It's like witnessing a birth."

"What?" Ricky says, convinced I've lost my mind.

"This doesn't upset me. It's, like I said, watching a birth."

There are these decisive moments in life when you know something has begun. I can't say when that was with Julia—the video the orphanage sent? The first time we met her? The night we spirited her away? I don't know. Seeing my house like this is one of those times.

On the drive up to Ellenville that night I see storm clouds gathering.

"What happens if it rains?" I ask.

"They'll cover the house with a tarp."

"Hmm." The house is no longer just a thing. It's become part of me.

"You know," I say, "I know we're not speaking to my parents and I'm happy to have it that way for now. But my dad would find this whole process fascinating."

"And your mother would find every way to let you know you've made a big mistake," he quips.

"So true."

∞∞∞

Every spare moment I have I work on the house. I lay out fifty paint chips across the floor and eliminate them one by one before deciding what color to paint a wall. I toil for hours on our dial-up computer, scrolling websites on bathroom sinks and lighting fixtures. We spend our weekends in the Catskills at kitchen-and-bathroom specialists, picking tiles and shades and appliances. Every day there's one glitch or another, but I soldier through because I'm determined to keep the contractors on schedule. I find myself thinking about Hurricane Katrina and its aftermath. I wish I could do something more than send money, like adopt a dog or even go down there, but I'm bringing a dead house back to life.

One Saturday afternoon, we return from Home Depot. The fall chill is settling in.

"Let's open the town," I say to Ricky and Julia.

The town is a comprehensive set of wooden blocks that are tiny replicas of houses and shops and public buildings. The set has mix-and-match roofs that remind me of the Beaux Arts architecture of the Upper West Side. There are plastic green trees and a yellow bus and red fire engine. Julia tears toward the cardboard box and rips at the plastic furiously. The pieces spill to the floor. I try to get her to play *with* me, but she wants to do her own thing. The blocks amuse her for less than ten minutes.

"Julia, wait. We've just started." She drifts away.

I'm about to toss the blocks aside and move on to my heady to-do list, but I sit down again. I put roofs on houses and string houses into streets and make streets cross with other streets where pedestrians find the post office and the hospital and the school. Then I add plastic green trees near the buildings and school buses and fire engines along the roads.

"You've done a fine job, Mama," Ricky says, standing behind me. "Julia, come look at the town Mama made."

Eighteen

"Julia, hurrr-ry up, we're waiting," Ricky calls, his hands cupped over his mouth like a megaphone. "I see Betty. There she is. She's waiting for you. C'mon."

Betty is our ketchup-red SUV.

"Can you see her?" I ask with a scowl, squinting to scour the shaded woody trail we've been walking for the past hour.

"She's playing her usual game," Ricky says.

By that he means she's hanging back thirty feet on the trail or hiding behind a wide tree or pretending she has a pebble in her shoe. This is what she does. Every time. Anything to control the pace and manipulate the mood of a family outing. We've been taking long walks with Julia since she was two. At three and a half, she's capable of hiking five forested, hilly miles. Her legs are solid slabs of muscle. She's a jaguar, built for endurance. She could be the world's tiniest Olympic athlete. We call her Bam Bam. She never breaks a sweat. On a long trek, she doesn't complain about fatigue; she doesn't raise her arms and whine "Hold me." What she does is stall and tarry and hide because it makes her feel powerful. Going along is out of the question. Harmony is abhorrent. No exceptions.

We've tried to encourage her to walk alongside us by playing word games or educating her about this bird or that berry. We bring apples and say, “We’ll eat them in twenty minutes,” hoping to dangle the proverbial carrot. Ricky says we should try donuts. And he’s probably right—I’ve seen the mothers who use sugar as their prime weapon. We grasp her hand, but she eludes us, Jell-O sliding through my fist. We sing. She won’t. She either runs far ahead or lags far behind. Her tactics frustrate Ricky. I beg him to stay patient.

“*Why?*” he says. “She makes this so unpleasant. What’s the point?”

“Think of it as a long-term investment,” I say. “It’s painful now, but one day this will be second nature to her. It’s something we can always do together as a family. Hiking is a ritual she’ll seek comfort in because she’ll associate it with something she’s always done.” Ricky is skeptical but willing to persist.

My mother never walked through the woods. She has never laced up a pair of hiking boots or climbed a steep trail to a plateau where the whole wide world is there for you to feast on. My family didn’t spend time together outdoors. We didn’t hike or camp or swim in lakes. My mother was a city girl, at home among concrete and chaos. My father was a hybrid. He spent his teen and adult years in Brooklyn, but as a young boy he was raised among immigrant farmers in northern Connecticut. Married to my strong-willed mother, who once said, “If you’ve seen one mountain, you’ve seen them all,” his intense desire for the natural world had to be sated with exotic images from *National Geographic* and from *Animal Kingdom* flickering on a thirteen-inch television on his bedroom dresser. Lucky for me, I got to go to sleepaway camp in the Catskill Mountains for a decade. I learned that the woods are the finest retreat when my heart is confused.

Ricky is tapping his muddy boot. Julia is dragging her feet; she’s wearing a smirk that says, *Look how clever I am for making you wait.*

“Maybe *we* should duck behind that tree—give her a taste of her own medicine,” I say. “If we disappear out of sight, maybe she’ll get a good scare.”

“I doubt it,” Ricky says.

“You’re probably right. Either she’s too smart for us, or she wouldn’t give a rat’s ass if we disappeared.”

Suddenly Julia sprints toward us. When she catches up, she doesn't stop. She slices by like an airborne razor boat skimming a lake.

"Juliiiaaaaa, stop!" Ricky yells.

She's hurtling over a green mound toward the parking lot.

She won't slow down. She won't acknowledge Ricky's pleas.

He scoots after her. After a couple of minutes, he gains a lead. And with plain intention, he sticks his boot in front of her shins and she topples forward onto the grass. I'm ten feet behind, but I see the whole thing. I'm stunned. Before I close in on them, I spot a man with a wild-eyed look clamoring up the knoll from the other direction, his arms winding like windmills. Julia is splayed on the ground, crying. Ricky lifts her up, brushing dirt off her knees.

The stranger is apoplectic.

"What the hell is wrong with you?" he shouts. "I saw what you did. She's only a little girl. Are you crazy?"

"Mind your business," Ricky barks back.

The guy continues yelling and shaking his head as he turns around and walks back to where he came from.

Julia is shell-shocked, but she's stopped crying. She's not hurt.

"Are you all right?" I say to Ricky. "Is she okay? What was that about?"

"I don't know," he says, looking dazed and ashamed. "I lost it. I saw her heading to the parking . . ."

"I understand," I say, stroking his arm. "She drives us to extremes."

"I shouldn't have done that," he says, looking ashen.

"Don't beat yourself up," I say. "I thought that man was going to slug you."

"He's an asshole." Ricky pauses. "Thing is, it's assholes like that who call the police. Before you know it you've got social services in your house. Nobody understands what we're dealing with."

"You're right. Nobody does. It's not your fault. Grab her hand. Let's go."

We are in the car heading back to Ellenville. Julia is merrily humming "Twinkle, Twinkle Little Star." The sun sags low in the sky. Parched leaves dangle languidly from naked tree branches. The last of the season, the ones that have endured. Ricky is staring ahead, concentrating on the road. He's quiet. For the first two years after we brought Julia home, I thought I was the only one in the world who experienced difficulties with her, that I'd made a mistake, that motherhood and I weren't meant to be. I told myself the problem is that she's not really mine and I had overestimated my ability to love and bond with a child who's not my flesh. Shame grew every day. Ricky's patience and tenderness with Julia offered some solace.

Then Julia had a nanny and subsequently she has started nursery school. A different picture started to emerge. Other adults found her difficult to manage. They had trouble hiding their exasperation. I recognized the forced smiles, the tiny blow of the lips that made a wisp of hair move. I knew the code phrases: *She certainly has a lot of energy. She's quite a fireball. Does she ever tire?*

But only in the last year have I seen Ricky become aggravated with her behavior. She's just as unresponsive to him as she is to me. He's described her as "feral"—which is a perfect description for a child who seems to need no one.

ᴑᴑᴑᴑᴑᴑ

In late July, when we temporarily relocated to Ellenville, I enrolled Julia in a nursery school six miles from the house we will live in soon. She's been there for three months, and it's not going well. I am often told she has trouble participating in circle time. She's been given several time-outs alone in the kitchen because she's disruptive in the dining room. The head mistress of the nursery school thinks it might be because I pack Julia's lunch for her every day. I don't bother to say, *I've walked through your kitchen and I'm not interested in feeding Julia the high-fructose, chemical-laden crap you serve.* It seems caretakers in institutions presume a child's difficult behavior is traceable to something the parents are doing. When Ricky drops Julia off in the morning, she clatters off without saying good-bye. When he or I pick her up, she is hiding under a desk, alone, filthy, and wild-eyed. Neutral at best about our arrival. There's an expression of relief on the teacher's face when we leave.

I can't put my finger on why this school is especially bad for Julia—worse than other group environments she's been in. Is it the transition from the city to the suburbs? Is it that the school is cheerless, cave-like, and somber? The rooms are underground. The lighting is poor. Even the backyard playground equipment is threadbare. Ricky thinks it's because the school doesn't hire trained professionals. "They hire on the cheap," he says, adding that Jocelyn, one of the two teachers, is essentially a babysitter. Julia, he says, has learned to "chew her up and spit her out." As she does with any adult who is yielding and soft.

One day while lamenting the nursery school situation, Ricky says, "You know, there's a pair of twins—well not really twins, brothers, who are a real handful also."

"Really?" I say.

"Yeah, Timmy and Kenny. Apparently they are both adopted from Russia. And I've heard through the grapevine they are a nightmare."

"Have you seen them?" I ask.

"I have. And here's the weird thing. They remind me of Julia. Same manic energy. Same faraway look in their eyes. Same craziness. When they see their dad at the end of the day they take turns saying, 'Hi Daddy, hi Daddy, hi Daddy, hi Daddy,' over and over. You know, the way Julia does."

"Wow," I say, contemplating the rare opportunity to meet someone who may know how I feel. "The next time we pick her up together, show me the brothers."

"I will."

∞∞∞

Morning temperatures in Ellenville plunge into the forties, though it's early October. The charming lake cottage is not so charming in winter's grip. We keep losing electricity, one time for a three-day spell. The utility company is in no rush to restore power to a desolate mountain road lined with summer bungalows. Yesterday we raided our rented storage room near our new house for sweaters and corduroy pants. Seeing our belongings for the first time in three months made me yearn to get our house finished and to move in. I spend every waking moment cracking the whip on painters, plumbers, carpenters, and electricians. Julia's unhappy days at nursery school loop through my mind and press on my heart. I need to find another school, but I must focus first on getting us settled.

One night it sounds like a sot is stumbling among glass bottles outside the window. I race to the window and squint. Blackness. In a hushed whisper, I call Ricky upstairs. He turns off the light and we return to the window. "Oh my God," I gush. "He's massive." *He* is a colossal, silver-eyed black bear who is erect on his hind legs and leaning on our car. "Oh my God," I keep saying. Ricky shines a flashlight into the bear's face. He sees us. No biggie. "Oh my God," is all I can say. Eventually he clatters away. I barely sleep that night. I'm jittery the next morning. Ricky, who comes in from outside, reports Mr. Hungry Bear left a swath of detritus. "I've tried to pick up what I can." We resume our routine and drive two hours to Nyack, where we drop Julia at nursery school. Ricky and I go off to work. I spend the day calling every subcontractor to keep each one on schedule. I worry about our cats alone in the flimsy cottage. When we return at night, I ask Julia and Ricky to make insane yodeling noises as we walk from the car to the house. Julia likes this. "I've heard that's the way to keep the bear away." In the days that follow, I throw every ounce of myself into making our move-in date Halloween, no matter how hard I have to fight and scream. The word "deadline" is not a word contractors know. I make a lot of people angry. I harass and harangue. I'm single-focused. I'm mama-bear, keeping me and my "cubs" from harm.

Miraculously, the badgering and persistence pays off. We leave Ellenville on Halloween and drive through a riot of autumn splash along the Palisades Parkway, before pulling into our driveway. Our driveway. I can't believe it!

∞∞∞

Julia's little girl bed looks like dollhouse furniture in her spacious, freshly painted pink room. Ricky had to slide a shim under her wooden dresser drawers because the hardwood floors slope. Gallons of light pour through four large windows. We bought Julia a painted toy chest that Ricky assembled and filled it to the brim. She has a little table with chairs. A surge of regret sears through me—*maybe if Julia had had a proper room from the start and I could have sat in a rocking chair and read to her.* I stop the thought. We are here now.

∞∞∞

Day after day I walk around the house in a reverie, amazed at what I've built. This old farmhouse, which was left to rot, is resuscitated and handsome. It holds my DNA. It is something I gave birth to. My genetic material resides in every tile, faucet, finish, light fixture, and shade of paint. This is how it feels to have something around me that reflects me. This is how a birth mother must feel when she arrives home from the hospital cradling her newborn.

∞∞∞

"Who were you on the phone with?" Ricky says, as he plops groceries on the glittering green granite counter.

"That was Julia's teacher Craig, again!" I say, with a frown.

"What's wrong this time?" he asks.

"Same old thing. Julia is acting up. She won't take instruction. Blah blah."

"What'd you say?" he asks.

"I just said, 'I see. I see.' But then he said something disturbing."

Ricky pauses from putting the groceries away and waits for me to continue.

"He asked if I wanted to have someone from the county come down and evaluate her. To see if she needed, I think he said, special services."

"What kind of special services?"

"I don't know. It didn't get that far. I was taken aback. I said I'd talk to you and get back to him."

We both recoil at the notion of letting some county bureaucrat "evaluate" Julia. Throughout the adoption process, we tolerated intrusion from home-study counselors, adoption workers, and the police who pressed our fingers in inky pads to capture our fingerprints to assure Russia we were not criminals. For months and years after the adoption, the agency would call from time to time, urging us to file reports. We never did. I was no longer willing to parent en masse.

Ricky thinks a visit like that ends up as a permanent record that will follow Julia through her life. He is skeptical a county counselor would have the skills to deal with our situation. So the uncomfortable thought hangs in the air, dangling like a phone receiver that bleeps annoyingly over and over off the hook.

Nineteen

His dinged jalopy kicks up dust in the driveway. He sticks his hand out the rolled-down window to open the car door, which is attached by the grace of duct tape, and then he springs from the car like a jack-in-the-box.

"Hi, I'm Christian," he says, extending his hand while a Cheshire cat smile spreads across his face.

I pump his hand.

He reaches into the car for cameras, a tripod, and lighting equipment.

He's instantly familiar from my decade spent with reporters and photographers in newsrooms. I recognize that boundless energy, the twinkle in his eye, an insatiable hunger to see inside people's souls. He's probably taken a million photographs during his career, but he shows up at my house with so much sunshine and gusto, you'd think this was his first assignment.

I lead him down the path to the house.

"This is quite the place you've got here. Wow!"

"It's my muse," I say, tossing that thought over my shoulder.

"We'll start inside," he says. "Then we can take some outdoor shots."

The *New York Post* has sent Christian to take photos of me and my family for a column I've begun writing. "Burb Appeal" is about the trials and tribulations of a hard-boiled city girl adjusting to life in her rural-ish suburb. It's about shock and awe. It's about leaving what is familiar and finding out who you really are. The first column will run in a few weeks with photos. This is a high point in my writing career.

Christian transforms our house into a studio. He tests lighting. He raises shades; he lowers them. He moves furniture. He stages. He suggests a mock tea session in the living room. "Can you add a book to that scene—pretend you're reading?" he directs. He talks to our cats when they wander by. He snaps me on the couch. "You've modeled before, right?" he says to flatter me, to cajole my come-hither glint. He's good. He photographs me in the kitchen handing Julia apple slices. She grabs them with delight and mugs for the camera in her pink stripy shirt and flared pink skirt that looks like a cheerleader's. Her socks have gone AWOL. Upstairs Christian captures Julia rolling around on her new wrought-iron bed under the pink-petaled floral comforter. He gets one of her pretending to serve food on plastic dishes from her make-believe kitchen and another of her lifting up her purple alphabet caterpillar. She likes this a lot. It's interesting to see her engaged in something. Then we go outside. Early spring flowers are muscling through the earth. Christian lines us up, one behind the other, sitting on a stone bench like a human caterpillar.

We are a caterpillar in its cocoon, hiding from the glare and scrutiny of the world. We cocoon ourselves because it's too hard to explain to others what we are. I don't speak to my mother. Or my father. Or my sister. We barely speak to Ricky's mother, and when we do we are careful to keep our troubles private. Old friends are far away, disembodied voices that have no real connection to my life. I don't tell them how disconnected I feel from my child or how devastating motherhood is. Or how I doubt that my relationship with Julia is ever going to fuse into something I don't think about on a philosophical level. Instead I talk about the house and the newspaper column, the things that work for me. I project a happy face to the world—just like my mother taught me to do. "Never let them know you're weak," she'd say. The people I see now are acquaintances from Julia's preschool or women from yoga class. I wait for a breakthrough, to be that caterpillar that pushes his way from the cocoon and becomes a brilliant flash of light and color. I gaze skyward while Christian checks his camera's digital monitor, and I speak to that invisible force out there who has some inkling as to how this is all going to play out. *Is it going to get better?* I ask silently. *When?*

Three hours glide by in the wink of an eye. As Christian walks up the driveway to his hopeful hunk of junk on wheels, we wave good-bye. I feel like we've spent a day with an old friend. Maybe it's the intimacy of being photographed? Maybe it's Christian's infectious nature?

∞∞∞

A couple of weeks later, a CD arrives in the mail. Christian has sent me fifty pictures from the shoot. I scroll through the staged version of my life. What is real? What truths does the camera tell? What does it hide? In most of the pictures, Julia appears to be an adorable almost-four-year-old despite the bad bangs chop, which is my fault. She is giggly and expressive. There's even one where I'm at the kitchen counter cutting fruit, Ricky is standing two feet away, and Julia is balancing herself on a little white stool in between us, one hand holding Ricky's, the other resting on my knee. Did Christian ask her to do that? Would she have leaned on me if he hadn't? But then I spot a couple of disturbing photos. In one, Julia is looking up at the camera from her bed, and her face reminds me of children I've seen at the orphanage, children who will never leave because they have fetal alcohol syndrome or other neurological issues. What brings them to mind is how thin her lips look and the way her eyes seem too widely spread apart.

∞∞∞

"That's him," Ricky says.

"That's who?" I ask.

"Timmy and Kenny's father. You know, the Russian brothers I told you about." It's Friday afternoon. We've just pulled into the preschool parking lot to pick up Julia to go out to dinner.

"Let's talk to him," I say.

He's an imposing man, suited and groomed. He's talking on his cell phone. He looks like he sells things. Ricky and I hang back until he stuffs his cell into his pocket.

"Hey, Jim," Ricky says.

"Oh, hey."

"Jim, this is my wife, Tina," Ricky says.

"Nice to meet you."

"Waiting for your boys?" Ricky says.

"Yup," he says.

He furrows his brow.

Because we have to get Julia shortly and because he'll soon be distracted with his boys, I brazenly jump in.

"I don't know if you know this, but Julia is from Russia. Ricky tells me your boys are also from Russia. Adopted, like Julia."

He hesitates for a minute.

"Uh, yeah." He recovers smoothly. "We adopted the boys at the same time. They're not biological brothers, but we wanted two children."

"Did you have to make two trips to Russia?"

"We did," he says.

"So did we. It's not an easy thing."

He's looking at me. Waiting for me to continue.

"It's just that . . . I don't know what it's like for you and your wife, but Julia is, let's just say, difficult. She's got issues. We don't really know anyone with adopted Russian children."

I wait with hopeful eyes.

Slowly, he warms.

"It's true. These guys are a handful. My wife and I are exhausted all the time. They're hyper and insatiable. They really thrive on chaos."

"I know, I know," I trill. "I know exactly what you mean. Chaos. The perfect word." I look at Ricky.

He's nodding.

"They run rings around us," Jim continues, "and they're difficult in school too, but we're doing our best to cope. What else can we do?"

"We're in the same boat," I say. "It's like there's never any peace . . ."

"Daddy." "Daddy." "Daddy." "Daddy." "Daddy."

Jim's head whips around. The two wiry boys are scaling him like he's their favorite backyard tree. Ricky shoots me the *See what I mean?* look. I do. These boys have that same feral look in their eyes as Julia. They are relentless and demanding and determined to ingest Jim's marrow. Jim apologizes and says, "Gotta go. We should talk more some other time."

Though it's nearly Memorial Day, the nights are cold in our old-but-renovated wooden farmhouse. In the city we lived in a prewar building with thick plaster walls. We had no control over the radiators, which pumped out heat through June. Even in winter, we'd keep the windows cracked open. Now I'm walking through the house wrapped in a sage-green alpaca blanket when Ricky shrieks, "Come here, come here."

He's propped himself up from the couch, staring in disbelief at the television screen.

"What is it?"

"Just come here, hurry."

A woman in orange-issue prison garb is telling her story to a female reporter. Natalia Higier is spending a year in prison for involuntary manslaughter of her two-year-old son adopted from Russia. The adoptive Massachusetts mother is recalling how she originally said her son, Zachary, who died from massive brain injuries, had fallen out of his crib and hit his head. And that she later changed her story, saying she threw him in the air—a game he loved—and he slammed his head on a coffee table. She is telling the dewy-eyed reporter she was lambasted for waiting two hours to take him to the emergency room. She was alone when all this happened. Tearfully, Natalia Higier concedes she did the wrong thing and she's paying for it. The boy, her son, was difficult to care for, she explains. She never really felt like his mother. Her husband was constantly away on business, and when she'd tell him how difficult it was to manage the child, he didn't believe her.

Natalia Higier was alone in the world. She had no one to confide in. She didn't even know how to ask for help.

If I were watching this interview four years ago, before I became Julia's mother or before I started down the road of adoption, I'd see a twisted monster on my television screen. I'd say this woman should have been better screened and, had that been the case, she never would have been allowed to adopt a baby boy. But this is not four years ago. This is May 2006, three years since Julia came home, and I understand this woman's plight. I know what it's like to have a child who doesn't feel like he or she is yours. I know what it's like to have a child who resists you, who never takes your hand or looks you in the eye or listens. I know this woman's daily struggle between the desire to love this blond boy and how difficult that is when what is returned amounts to indifference. I get how a woman who is forty-seven years old, who ran a business, and loved her dog, could become so inconsolable that she becomes unhinged. How too many consecutive days of relentless isolation and despair can lead to violence. How there's nothing left to lose.

When the program ends, Ricky and I hold each other. I'm shaking.

"Could that ever be me?" I ask, tearfully.

"Of course not," he says.

"That's because I have you," I say. "That woman was all alone in the world."

"It's true," he says. "It sounds like she was struggling by herself and snapped."

"The world condemns a woman like that. Which I understand. There was a time I would have been scornful too."

"Yeah, but now you—we—know what this woman's life was probably like. This is a problem. I bet many parents with Russian children are struggling behind closed doors. There's so much shame around this."

"Exactly," I say, stabbing my finger in the air. "Nobody can fathom that a child may be unlovable. It's got to be the parents who are damaged."

"Well, maybe a program like this shows people a different side to the story, though I doubt it. They probably air stories like this because they are sensational. Anyway, let's go upstairs. It's getting late."

"I need a few minutes," I say.

I walk to my desk and type in "Natalia Higier and Russian adoption" on my keyboard.

As the pages load, Ricky leans over my shoulder and says, "I bet there are more cases like this. A lot more cases."

"Oh my God," I gasp.

"What is it?"

"Well, for one thing the Higiers used the same adoption agency as we did. Look here. It says, 'The state Department of Child Care Services will investigate to make sure that the Frank Adoption Center used a Massachusetts-licensed adoption agency to conduct the home study and background.'"

"Whoa. What else?"

"According to this story, the couple had a home study, and everything checked out. But listen to this. There's a lawyer from the adoption agency quoted here saying, 'This family was very well suited to adopt a child.'"

"What else?"

"Hang on. . . . Okay, listen to this. This is from the director of the Center for Family Connections in Cambridge, the people who did their home study. They say, 'Often parents who adopt foreign children may not be prepared to take care of a child who may have been abandoned or malnourished or lived in an orphanage.'"

"Yeah, well, they certainly don't tell you that when you're plonking down $40,000 to adopt a child," Ricky says. "Let's go upstairs."

I toss and turn all night, imagining what it's like to accidentally or maybe intentionally be driven to the point where a mother kills her child. It makes me ache. I picture Julia, across the hall, sleeping in her bed. Julia, Zachary. Unwanted children who are severed from a mother's love and sent to live in orphanages like dogs and cats to the pound. Only their absolute needs are met—and not necessarily in a timely or loving way. And we adoptive mothers believe we can cure them with our love, but it's not a medicine they're willing to swallow. Poor little Zachary. Unwanted. Disconnected. Dead. A footnote in history.

Twenty

I tiptoe downstairs, trying not to wake Ricky or Julia. I cinch my robe tightly because the heat hasn't kicked on yet and the house still feels like a meat locker in early June. I rarely have time for myself in the morning. Julia rises at the crack of dawn every day, like a rooster. I raise the kitchen shades and stare into the milky light. I cannot stop thinking about Zachary or Natalia. I saw the clock every two hours last night, tossing like a fish gasping for air in a waterless bucket.

I flip on the kettle and spoon loose-leaf tea into a cup. The three cats mewl at my ankles, pressing up against me to fill their food and water bowls. Their sweet faces deflect my dark thoughts for a fleeting second, but then I am again picturing how Natalia must have panicked when she realized Zachary was unconscious. What was it like for her in the moment she understood the situation had gone too far? Was she scared? Remorseful? Relieved? In some dark corner of her mind, I wonder, was she relieved she would not have to be Zachary's mother anymore? Was living with the child a worse prison sentence than the one she's serving now? The kettle's wet plume of steam fogs the window. I pour boiling water into my cup and carefully carry it into my office.

I type "Russian Adoption" and "Death" into Google. I hesitate, fortify myself with a sip of tea and hit "Enter." I cup my hands around the hot mug to warm me. I'm chilled inside and out. Scary words appear in a long list on my screen. Russian adoption and death are not strangers. I suck in my breath as I click on a link titled "Russian Child Murder Cases."

Someone has published a list—*a list!*—of twelve Russian adoptees who've, as the list says, "died at the hand of their US adoptive parents." The list is arranged in paragraphs, each citing the child's name, age at the time of death, legal words about the crime, and how long the child had been living in his adoptive home. I look at the names and ages first. They're American names mostly, changed, but in some cases their former Russian name is cited. There's "David, age 2," "Logan, age 3," "Viktor, age 6," "Luke, age 18 months," "Jacob, age 5."

Then I come to Zachary. Natalia's son. It says, "Zachary, age 2, of Braintree, Massachusetts, died of severe head trauma. Zachary sustained a bilateral skull fracture, strokes, brain swelling, and detached retinas." The paragraph concludes with, "Natalia pleaded guilty to involuntary manslaughter and is serving jail time," as I already know. My heart breaks for the baby and for her, too. I see her in my mind's eye with a child who is as wild and depraved as a rabid raccoon. She's supposed to love this little boy, but she can't. In lucid moments, she assuages herself by believing things will improve with time. He'll calm down. Zachary will let her be his mother. But in a cold, stark, unbearable moment, where she is just as out of control as the baby, Zachary ends up dead. What actually happened? Only Natalia knows. It doesn't matter now.

I hear Julia and Ricky stirring upstairs, but I'm frozen stiff in front of my computer screen. Emotional rigor mortis has set in. I should start making breakfast, but the revelations on the screen chain me to my chair. I scroll again to the top of the page, this time to read the actual story of each and every child: David and Logan and Viktor and Luke and Jacob. I skip past Zachary's story to Maria's, Jessica's, Liam's, Alex's, Dennis's, and Nina's. Horrific, unimaginable deaths. There's something unfathomable about a tiny child being killed.

How is it that we have been through the adoption process and no one whispered a word of this dark underbelly to us? Is it a coincidence that this many cases of Russian adoptions turned bad?

These adoptive parents who stand accused and convicted went through a rigorous, exhaustive, and expensive process to adopt a child from Russia. Did any of them start off with malice in their heart? Did they sit down and say, "Hmm, let's forfeit our life's savings and spend a year drowning in bureaucracy and travel to Russia twice so we can abuse a child"? Did home study guidance counselors miss telltale clues about these people as prospective parents? They couldn't see these folks would have a predilection to harm children? I don't buy it. There's more to this. I think Irma and Donna and Peggy and Kimberly were drowning in confusion and despair and feelings of unbearable inadequacy. At some point that lethal cocktail of emotions led to a strike or a blow that couldn't be taken back.

If you're standing back from a cool, objective distance, you might think, *Well, if I had a child like that, I'd get her help.* I'd think that too. But I understand *The Twilight Zone* of Russian adoption because I live it. Being unable to bond with a baby isn't the same as having an adolescent who is experimenting with drugs or running away from home and deciding it's time to seek help. An adoptive parent with no prior knowledge of this down-the-rabbit-hole world doesn't understand how a baby can be so disturbed. A mother figures enough love and time will fix the problem, that the slate's still blank. She doesn't believe a baby can be so damaged—or evil. There is Renee Polreis, who was convicted of child abuse and sentenced to eighteen years in prison for the death of David Polreis Jr. In the paragraph on her case, she said her baby's cuts were self-imposed and due to severe RAD. Reading the acronym "RAD," I wonder if she knew what that was at the time or whether it was a phrase she learned when she was mounting a defense.

I hear Julia and Ricky clattering down the steps. I close the screen quickly, as though I'm reading something illicit. Ricky pops into my office.

"What are you doing up so early? You look like you've seen a ghost."

"Twelve of them."

"What?"

"I'll explain later. Let's get breakfast started. Is Julia dressed and ready for school?"

"Mostly."

At breakfast I watch Julia shovel cereal into her mouth. Her face is practically in the bowl. She chews loudly while rice milk seeps out of the corners of her mouth. Bits of oats stick to strands of silky golden hair. She doesn't look at me or Ricky. She doesn't clean her face with a napkin unless told to do so.

"Julia, wipe your face," Ricky says, handing her a napkin. She hesitates a moment, watching us watch her. Then she dabs her chin, and looks back up at Ricky with her eyes narrowed, waiting to be told to do it again. I can see the satisfied expression ooze across her face. When that's done, she gulps her juice loudly and deliberately, like a dehydrated fireman replenishing himself after escaping a burning building. Usually I find the "eating game," as Ricky and I call it, repulsive. Today I'm gazing at her with deep concern, and my eyes water.

"What's going on with you?" Ricky asks.

"I have to show you something."

We send Julia upstairs to play with LEGO blocks. "Build a castle," Ricky says as she stomps up the steps. We know she's not likely to stay put for long. I rush over to the computer, recover the screen and say, "Look!" Ricky bends over my shoulder to see the list of murdered Russian children. "Let me sit down," he says, gently evicting me from my computer chair. He leans toward the screen. His eyes dart back and forth quickly. Every few seconds, he glances over his shoulder.

"Where's Julia?" he asks.

"Still upstairs playing LEGOs."

"This is stunning," he says.

"I know. It's insane. Do you think all these parents deliberately set out to abuse or murder their children?" I ask, shaking my head in disbelief.

"Of course not. I think people like us who adopt Russian children have no idea what they're getting themselves into."

"Like us? Could this happen to us, to me?"

"Don't be silly. I know you're frustrated and unhappy and you're worried sick, but you're not violent. Besides, she's so physically powerful she would probably hurt you before you could hurt her."

Ricky's jesting, but there's truth in what he says. At times, I am actually afraid of Julia's incredible physical strength.

"Notice how it's always the mother, not the father, who commits the act," I say. "And look at those prison terms: a year, five years, eighteen years! My God! This is awful."

"It's because no one prepares us or tells us what to expect. Maybe some adoptive parents are briefed, or maybe they know they need to research this, but I bet most are like us. All they think about is bringing home the child. That's what we were thinking about when we were going through the process."

"So true. Look at that one," I say, pointing to Jessica Albina Hagmann's name."

Whispering aloud I read, "The mother claimed she accidentally killed Jessica while trying to stop her from having a tantrum."

"Remember that child on the plane home from Russia?" Ricky says, waiting for me to recall. "You know, the one who sat opposite us. She was about twenty months or so. Remember how she was wailing and rolling on the floor for the better part of the ten-hour flight? I imagine a child like that becomes Jessica Albina Hagmann."

We hear Julia on the steps.

"She's coming down," I say.

"I'll run her down to school. We can talk about this later."

∞∞∞

I know I should get on with my day. I have so much work, but I can't tear myself away from this list. I keep going. I type each child's name in Google and piece together how each of these tragedies unfolded in online clips I find in local newspapers. I crave to know what happened in unhappy houses in Colorado, Vermont, Indiana, Ohio, Illinois, Maryland, and

North Carolina. I want to find a pattern. One that makes sense. One that tells me this will never be me. But I can't. These are ordinary people who adopted babies from Russian orphanages, and there are many of them. "This is not a coincidence," I say to myself. I log off.

The blue sky fills up the world outside my large picture window. I see Ricky standing akimbo at the other end of our property pondering God only knows what. Surviving our first winter on the mountain taught us we live on a treacherous road that becomes impassable in the snow and that it's nearly impossible to get a car out of the driveway. When the snow melted, we discovered six concrete cisterns perched dangerously in our woods. They were used to capture rainwater a century ago, but we had to call in a stonemason to crush them up and haul them away because they were an eyesore and a danger. We learned the maple trees bloom first and the catalpas are still bare until late June. And the nutty professor who lived in what was barely a house for seventeen years before us scattered tin cans of cat food for strays and that she, and the inhabitants before her, never took the time to plant gardens.

"Julia, come with me," I say, trying to grasp her hand.

She pulls it away. It's like trying to hold a birder dog chasing a sparrow.

"Come on, I want to see what Daddy's up to."

I have to grip her arm tightly to get her to walk outside with me. She runs ahead toward Ricky. He catches her, as though I'd thrown a ball.

"What are you doing? Or should I say what are you *thinking*?" I ask.

"I'm going to pull out all the weeds and brush from this patch and make a vegetable garden."

I stifle a laugh.

"How? This is not a 'patch.' It's like an acre of garbage."

"I know. I know. One weed at a time. You'll see. By July we'll have tomatoes and peppers and cucumbers."

"Are you planning on getting a team of oxen?"

"Go ahead. Make fun. You have no faith. You'll see."

"No, no. Knock yourself out. I don't want to discourage you. It just seems like an awesome task."

"Isn't everything we take on?"

I walk back to the house to prepare lunch. His words linger . . . "Isn't everything we take on?" He's right. The two of us have tackled more in the six years we've spent together than I imagine many couples do. We've dealt with financial woes, unemployment, nearly losing the apartment sale, challenging family relationships, two trips to Siberia, and the complete renovation of a derelict farmhouse. And our biggest challenge—being Julia's parents.

∞∞∞

After a week, Ricky has transformed himself into a human thresher. His arms are pricked with cuts from thistles. But he has miraculously carved a clearing and he is building raised beds, filling them with soil, and enclosing them inside a chicken-wire fence.

On the morning of Mother's Day, a day that is always difficult for me, he takes Julia to Home Depot so I can get an extra hour of rest. We don't have any specific plans today, which is okay but somehow it feels like it shouldn't be. This is my fourth Mother's Day as a mother. It is difficult to cope with my feelings about being a daughter, and it's equally sticky to feel celebrated as a mother. I'm an imposter in both roles. I'll call my mother today because I have to. We'll both follow the rules. I'll say, "Happy Mother's Day." She'll say, "Thank you." Neither will ask the other how each is spending the day. I'll try to get off the phone quickly as soon as the silence sets in. She'll breathe a long, exasperated sigh into the receiver and say, "Enjoy your day," which she surely doesn't mean. And she will not say "Happy Mother's Day" back to me, to acknowledge that I, too, am a mother. This chill might be more bearable if I felt at ease at being Julia's mother, but I don't.

"Mommy, Mommy, Mommy, come and see what we got," Julia says, rocking my shoulder as I lie sloth-like on the bed.

I open my eyes. Julia and Ricky hover over me.

"C'mon," Ricky says. "Get up. Get some clothes on. Here, put this on."

"C'mon, Mommy, c'mon."

I toss off the covers. Ricky and Julia wait while I dress.

They each take one of my hands and lead me outside, up the path to Ricky's garden. I can't see where I'm being taken because Julia has insisted I keep my eyes closed. We stop at the top of the hill. "Okay, Mommy, open your eyes." Ricky hands me a trowel and says, "Happy Mother's Day!" At my feet are scores of tiny, hopeful tomato, cucumber, and pepper seedlings poking out of peat cups. I'm like a giant in a miniature forest. There are also trays of green sprigs labeled basil, dill, and Italian parsley.

"Let's get our hands dirty," Ricky says.

I hesitate for a moment because I've never planted a garden. Then I step into the spongy soil bed and kneel down low. Ricky shows me how to dig a small hole in the warm soil. Then he demonstrates how to twist and squeeze the plant from the peat cup. It feels like squeezing a pea from a pod. He shows me how to situate the tiny plant in the soil and to get it to stand straight by building a mound of dirt around it with my cupped hands.

"Let me know when you've planted a row," he says. "I'll come back with water."

He takes Julia by the hand and leaves me to plant.

The sun has warmed the earth, and the scent of dirt rises gloriously into my nose and intoxicates me. I don't even bother to wear the cotton gardening gloves he bought for me because it is such a pleasure to thread my hands through the loamy soil. I'm caked in dirt. I feel like a child who is finger painting. Messy. Surprised by swirls of color. Sure that something beautiful and ripe will emerge. My husband and daughter went to the Home Depot nursery this morning and brought me back a metaphor. Nurture something, and eventually it will bear fruit.

OOOOOO

The humid room is packed. We're lucky to find a couple of free chairs in the back. Not long after we arrive, parents are lining up along the walls. Many are fiddling with video cameras, testing the angles. I know from previous events like this that Julia will not know the songs or the hand movements. I suffer when I watch her on stage and she looks lost. That's what I've come to expect from these nursery school concerts, so I'm antsy. Ricky leans in to whisper "keep your expectations low."

"I know," I say. "I know the drill."

The children march onto a three-tiered stage. Julia is always in the front because she's pint-sized compared to the rest. Ricky and I wave to her. She looks frozen. As the songs get underway, I see her fidgeting. Predictably, she is not singing. But she looks more agitated than she usually does in situations like this. By the second song, I see her vying for her teacher Jocelyn's attention. Jocelyn is sitting in the front row, trying to get Julia to focus. I see Jocelyn's arms waving and then she reaches out to steady Julia on the stage. There is some commotion. I can't exactly see what's going on, but my tumbling stomach tells me it's not good. I look up again, and Jocelyn is removing Julia from the stage, trying to appease her with a stuffed bear. The children continue to perform. A couple of parents turn and offer a sympathetic look. They're probably thinking, *Julia's having a bad day. It's not a big deal. Things like this happen.*

I start to stand up, but Ricky pulls me down.

"Wait for the concert to end. I'm sure she's all right."

At this moment, I know in my heart she's not all right and I must do something about it. This is my child. She's calling out for help. I must come to her aid. Once and for all.

When the concert ends, I push past the crowd to find Jocelyn and Julia. Julia looks content and perky, as though nothing unusual had transpired.

"What happened?" I ask Jocelyn.

"I don't know. She was kinda having a meltdown on the stage."

"Do you know why?"

"No, I'm not really sure. But she seems fine now."

There's a stampede to a table spread with cupcakes and apple juice. "I want a cupcake, Mama," Julia says. Ricky helps her with a snack.

∞∞∞

On the ride home, I fight tears. Ricky squeezes my knee. But when we get to the house, I tell him to go inside without me. I open the wooden-framed chicken-mesh door and step into the garden. I sit down next to my promising plants. I'm sobbing so audibly it sounds like I'm listening to someone else. The sun shines around me, and the earth smells like heaven. How cruel it is when the world around me looks beautiful, but my child is lost.

I dry my tears and walk back to the house.

"I was worried about you."

"We've got to do something," I say. "We've got to help her. Before it's too late."

PART THREE

Make Love Happen

Twenty-one

My hands hover over the computer keyboard. They are trembling. I hold down the shift key and type the letters "RAD." Before I can bear to look at the search findings, I quickly tap the backspace key and erase the letters. I close my eyes and draw a deep breath. I have been tested many times in my life. I possess a profound inner strength, and I am even stronger because of the love I receive from Ricky. I type again, this time spelling it with intention, saying each letter aloud: "R-e-a-c-t-i-v-e A-t-t-a-c-h-m-e-n-t D-i-s-o-r-d-e-r." Speaking the words makes them real. Reactive Attachment Disorder. The first step breaks inertia's deadly choke hold.

The words "Reactive Attachment Disorder" are memory beads I gather into a pile and attempt to string along on a necklace. I think back to that first time I heard Barbara's husband mention it in Siberia when Barbara was in the midst of a meltdown I couldn't understand. She was afraid her baby would have trouble bonding. Her husband had told Ricky and me that Barbara thought Brandon might have Reactive Attachment Disorder because he wasn't making eye contact.

Not long after, Judith, my neighbor who is a psychiatrist, offhandedly threw out the term the first time she met Julia. We were talking about babies who start their lives in orphanages, and she mentioned the disorder. She wasn't suggesting that Julia showed any signs, but she'd said it was a well-known problem with children who'd been adopted from Romanian orphanages in the '80s and '90s. I remember nodding my head and thinking, *We got Julia young. It shouldn't be an issue. Shut up, Judith. Go home!*

Then, when I raised concerns with Dr. Traister about Julia's elusive but controlling behavior when she was a toddler, he also mentioned Reactive Attachment Disorder. Did I want a referral to a therapist, he wanted to know. No, I wanted to be like the other mothers sitting in his waiting room, worrying about a sniffle. Now I remember something he said: *The signs of Reactive Attachment Disorder usually reveal themselves fully when a child reaches five or six years old and they start having trouble in school settings.*

But Natalia Higier, that canary in the mineshaft, that ghost of Christmas past, she's the one who reached out from the television in her jailhouse jumpsuit and put her hands around my neck and said, *Get help now, before it's too late for your child and for you. Before you end up like me.*

When is it too late for a relationship to establish or to reestablish? When I married the first time, at twenty-six years old, I believed in unconditional love. I really did. I assumed my mother would always love and adore me, and I thought the same about my first husband. I thought I'd always reciprocate their love. Divorce altered my thinking. I called it "my mental apocalypse" because it brought a cleaver down on just about everything I had once believed. I did not love the man I'd married, and he didn't love me. Love was finite. Even more shocking was that my mother and I seemed to stop loving one another. At first I thought it was going to be a temporary bad spell, but our relationship kept deteriorating. Now it barely exists. A mother's love, badly broken, may be beyond repair. Am I in that situation with my daughter? She was cut off at birth from nurture and love. There was no one there to soothe her. Just because I want to love her doesn't mean she'll let me—or let anyone. But I will do everything I can to make love happen between Julia and me.

I retrain my eyes on the computer screen. There are scores of hits on "Reactive Attachment Disorder." I could scroll for days and there would still be things to read. I click through to the Mayo Clinic website. It says, "Reactive Attachment Disorder is a rare but serious condition in which infants and young children don't establish healthy bonds with parents or caregivers. A child with Reactive Attachment Disorder is typically neglected, abused, or orphaned. Reactive Attachment Disorder develops because the child's basic needs for comfort, affection, and nurturing aren't met, and loving, caring attachments with others are never established. This may permanently change the child's growing brain, hurting the ability to establish future relationships."

I read the paragraph twice, then a third time. Can Reactive Attachment Disorder be treated? Can it go away?

∞∞∞

I'm remembering something. When the adoption agency sent us Julia's grainy video, the counselor repeatedly used the phrase "she's an orphanage favorite." When I asked what that meant, she said that because Julia was especially beautiful and animated, she enjoyed special attention from her caregivers. "This is a good thing," she'd assured me. What she was really saying, in code—not that I realized it at the time—was that Julia was more likely to bond with adoptive parents because she was accustomed to attention and affection. It would have been better if the counselor had asked me if I understood the risks of adopting a child who'd begun life in an orphanage. I rub my temples. Another memory floats up. The fleshy babushka caregiver in the orphanage bouncing and coddling Julia in her arms while smiling slyly at me. She said something to Olga. Olga translated: "They will miss her. She's a favorite." I didn't pick up on how Olga in Siberia and my adoption counselor in North Carolina happened to use the same phrase. At the time the comment made me happy. She is a "favorite!" Now I whisper, "Bullshit." It's a game.

∞∞∞

I go back to the page. This is what it says: "The core feature [of Reactive Attachment Disorder] is severely inappropriate social relating which can manifest in two ways:

"1. Indiscriminate and excessive attempts to receive comfort and affection from any available adult, even relative strangers. 2. Extreme reluctance to initiate or accept comfort and affection, even from familiar adults, especially when distressed."

Bingo! I've often seen this behavior in Julia: she wants to be in control, and she's more interested in manipulating than in truly relating. In public, Julia is the waving beauty queen, the mayor of wherever, the cheerful, friendly, squeezable, adorable mascot. She runs to adult strangers, hugs them, works the room. She solicits their attention and wraps them around her tiny, agile fingers. She's good at it. As for children, she shows little interest in them.

Strangers or fleeting caretakers tell me I have the most adorable, delicious, precocious, confident child. Some say she's the most adorable, delicious, precocious, confident child they've *ever* encountered. I nod and smile and pretend to share their sentiment. I keep my knowing mother thoughts to myself. How can I explain to a stranger that at home this child is distant, elusive, emotionally closed off, and defiant? What stranger will not say, or at least think silently, *Really? I don't see that. It must be you because she's not like that with me.*

I keep reading. Page after page, document after document. I'm so engrossed I can't leave my seat and go to the bathroom. My backside has gone numb. I let all phone calls go to voicemail. The documents mimic one another. In nearly all, there's a list of behaviors RAD children display. Like anyone who has ever had a persistent stomachache or something similar, there's an urge to type in symptoms and self-diagnose on the Internet. By the time you've typed in your symptoms, you could have anything from a bug to cancer, so you learn to resist this exercise.

But the list I'm looking at is uncanny. If I had been asked to describe Julia, this is the list I would have come up with independently. The child is "superficially charming and engaging, particularly among strangers she feels she can manipulate." I'm thinking about the swim instructor at the Y who felt compelled to take Julia for a bathroom run twice during every one of her thirty-minute weekly swim lessons even though we had told the instructor time and again that Julia had been to the bathroom before the group lesson.

Next, the lists say the child "doesn't have close friends." One day, Ricky saw I was trying to play "dolls" with Julia, but I couldn't get her to role-play. He'd casually said, "Maybe she doesn't know how to play with someone else." At the time I said, "hmmm," and thought it must be me. Maybe I didn't have my heart in it, and Julia sensed it. I realize now it was a brilliant observation. Julia can keep herself entertained, perhaps longer than a "normal" four-year-old, but the only way she can "play" with someone else is to direct or orchestrate. It is never give-and-take, never back-and-forth. It's why Barbara freaked out when Brandon wouldn't play peek-a-boo. She knew what to look for.

"Doesn't make eye contact. Has a severe need to control everything and everyone. Is hypervigilant. Is hyperactive. Is lazy performing tasks. Has trouble understanding cause and effect. Has poor impulse control. Chatters incessantly." Uncanny!

I'm often asked by a teacher or babysitter, "Does she ever stop talking?" I smile a Botox smile because they think Julia is simply a chatty, precocious child. But it's not like that. She chatters from the moment she wakes to the moment sleep steals her from her worn-out vocal chords. She chatters incessantly at the table, in the car, while she's playing. She escalates the chatter when Ricky and I start to have a conversation or when the phone rings and I answer it. She uses the chatter to control her environment.

Ricky has a theory about it. He thinks Julia chatters constantly to soothe herself, to make herself feel present. He thinks silence and stillness scare her because she's afraid of her internal thoughts. Afraid to be, not *by* herself, but *with* herself. This is a fascinating theory because it reminds me of my mother, who also has the need to manufacture noise because she too fears her inner world.

The problem with living with the endless loop of chatter is that it's hypnotic. Sometimes it even makes me sleepy. I'm not kidding. But also I've learned to tune it out and so if and when there is a moment of lucid substance, there's a decent chance I'll miss it. Ironically, or maybe not so ironically, when Ricky and I try to have a pointed conversation with Julia, she will say "What? What?" She averts her eyes. She pretends not to hear the question. She turns the exchange into a power play.

Thwack. The mail truck has come. I push myself back from the desk and grab my keys. The white light of the near-summer sun makes me squint. A row of purple irises are abloom. I stick my nose into the fancy flower. They smell like bubble gum. It's hard to be pessimistic when roses are climbing the fence and a rabbit nips at the fringes of your vegetable garden. I grab the wad of mail and head back to the house.

I return to the list on my screen. So far the first eighteen traits are a perfect match. But then I see other characteristics that absolutely don't describe Julia. She is not "cruel to animals." She has not shown any "fascination with fire, blood, and gore or an interest in weapons." She is not "self-destructive," and even though she does not take care of her possessions herself and she does not show any affection or pride of ownership for a favorite toy or teddy bear, she's not intentionally destructive in our house. Nobody has suspected she has any "developmental or learning delays" and she doesn't "steal or lie."

∞∞∞

My head is spinning. I reach for the phone.

"You busy?"

"What's up?"

"I've spent the last three hours reading up on Reactive Attachment Disorder."

"And?"

"There's a ton of information about this on the Internet. A ton. It's overwhelming."

"What did you find?"

"Well, there are several sites on RAD. Each site lists characteristics of children with RAD, and what I'd say is that most of the descriptions on the lists really describe Julia to a T."

"Like what?"

"Okay. Let me read this to you."

I go down the list, reading slowly, one trait at a time. When I finish he emits a heavy breath.

"What do you think?" I ask.

"I don't know what to think. Like you said, it sounds like a list we could have made."

"I know," I say. "On one hand, it's upsetting. But on the other, I feel a weird sort of comfort. Like, it's not my fault. There's a reason things are as they are."

I tell Ricky that the research says young children who were cut off from their mothers early in their lives display these kinds of behaviors because they instantly learn the world is a cold, untrustworthy, uncaring place, even if they've had a caregiver. They feel like this because most of their urgent needs either had to wait or were never met.

"So now what?" he asks.

"I don't know. I think we should read what I've found on the Internet together, tonight. I'll print out a bunch of stuff. And then, maybe on Friday night instead of a movie, we should head to the bookstore and see what we can find."

"Sounds like a good plan. Talk to you later."

I glance at the clock. It's 2:00 PM. I have three hours before Julia needs to be picked up at school. I must process some of this. I walk upstairs to my bedroom and gather my swim gear. I will drive to the Y. Before I head downstairs, I go into Julia's room. My eyes travel along the bookshelves, which are lined with tattered picture books and framed pictures of Julia. I run my hand along the shelf to fix a frame that's toppled over and feel something obstructing it. I reach a bit further and clasp something leathery. I lift it up. It's one of her white, worn baby shoes with the multicolored shoelace holes. I clutch the shoe against my heart and sob.

∞∞∞

I slice through the cool water. My body feels more vulnerable because my heart is hurting. But the determination of pumping blood, of going back and forth until thirty minutes elapses, of fighting for breath, reminds me that life is always a struggle. But I push past discomfort. I focus on one thing only. I can make change. This is my child. I'm all she has. I have to make love happen between Julia and me.

Twenty-two

"What time did you tell Alison we'd be back?" Ricky asks about the babysitter, steering our car along a turtle-speed route lined with neon-lit strip malls, gas stations, and auto showrooms.

"Around 10-ish. Let's go to the bookstore first. Then we can grab a bite," I say.

"I'm gonna go to the Barnes & Noble in Nanuet. It's easier to park there than at Palisades. Friday night is a nightmare at the mall."

"That's okay, we've already been to the one at the mall."

For the past two weeks, I've done nothing but read everything there is to read online about Reactive Attachment Disorder. New Google searches—no matter how I duck-duck-goose the search words—bring me back to research I've already seen. From what I gather, psychologists believe Reactive Attachment Disorder is a legitimate dysfunction that affects children whose maternal bonds were severed or grossly compromised early on. There is a chorus of voices who debunk it; they say it's a made-up diagnosis. But those who treat it as a viable disorder say a child's brain gets rewired when her basic needs have not been met or are screwed with. They say the brain actually changes physiologically when children suffer this kind of deprivation. The most compelling studies on the disorder are about Romanian orphans who were adopted in the early 1990s after Nicolae Ceausescu's repressive regime was toppled by the

Romanian people. Not all, but many afflicted orphans are cold, violent, and detached. Adopting them has been a problem.

∞∞∞

Parents going through the adoption process are warned that a child who has begun life in an orphanage may be delayed. Ricky and I had steeled ourselves for the likelihood that Julia would need extra time to sit, crawl, walk, speak, potty train. I remember Olga explaining how orphans have low muscle tone because they are confined in cribs or on indoor swings for long periods of time. Julia, a Lilliputian Olympian, hasn't missed a cue. She sat up on her own days after we brought her home. She crawled shortly after that. She walked at twelve months, ran a minute later. She started making words at a year. She potty trained herself—and I mean *herself*—within a week of her second birthday. Her teeth grew in before many of the other toddlers' teeth did in her playgroup, though the front ones were rotten from decay and lack of calcium. She has never been challenged in motor skills or coordination or cognitive ability. Julia's been on the fast track. The only "delay" she had was growing in her silky, wheat-colored mop. She was bald until eighteen months, but I wasn't too worried. I bought her cute hats.

At every turn, I told myself that this child is okay—she must be okay. She's met every milestone. At the same time, she was detached. I don't know how a normal toddler reacts when a parent is ailing, but when I'm balled up on the couch in extreme menstrual pain, which happens every month and goes on for days at a time and I'm sick like the dickens, Julia shows no concern or empathy. Is that normal? As she got older, she showed constant opposition to everything, anything. She has a dire need to be in control. She will spite herself just to be in control. If I ask Julia to bring me something, say a book, she makes me wait and wait. She dallies or slows down the process of a simple task just to keep me—or anyone—hanging. She enjoys hearing a second request and then a third more impatient one. When I lose patience and get up and get the book myself, she smirks.

Many times Ricky has said to her, "You know, Julia, it takes more energy to be mean than it does to be nice."

She'll outgrow this spitefulness, I told myself. *She will, she will, she has to.* In my logical mind I could not understand why she wasn't making a connection between positive deeds and positive reinforcement compared to disapproval following rebellious behavior. Now I understand. Kids with RAD are extremely challenged when it comes to connecting cause and effect. But there's another explanation, too. Julia is afraid of the warm and fuzzies. Good, loving deeds are rewarded with smiling faces and loving embraces, and if you're scared to death of intimacy and harmony, there's no good reason on earth to court it. I'm starting to get it. I've got my own cause-and-effect explanation to wrap my head around. I can stop being angry at Julia. I don't have to be disappointed in myself. Julia's actions are a camouflage for fear.

I understand fear. It is crippling and consuming. Fear permeates my bones, my thoughts, and my nighttime dreams. Ricky says I cling to fear like it's a life raft. I need it. I rely on it. It's familiar. He calls it "my friend." I wouldn't know who I am without anticipating some kind of disaster or loss. Fear and I have a bargain worked out. We need each other. I've worked in the news business for decades. The bad news business. Loss—random, horrific, tragic loss—is what we cover day in and day out. I've covered floods and train wrecks and inner city murders and kidnappings. I've covered good things too, but they don't lodge in my psyche the same way.

Ricky doesn't buy it. He says those are things that have happened to other people.

"Okay," I say. "Maybe it's because my dog died suddenly from a terrible cancer or because I've learned love doesn't last or because at seventeen I aborted the only baby my body will ever bring into this world."

Ricky smiles at me in that way that makes it impossible for me to stay mad. He wants me to be at peace. I struggle to understand his Zen, considering the fact that he has known loss, lots of it. But it doesn't bog him down. He doesn't think each new day will conjure a tragic headline. Studying Reactive Attachment Disorder makes me think about my own nature and my early childhood. Maybe I was starved of some needed nurture or attention. My mother must have been preoccupied with her difficult marriage. And I was always refereeing between my father and grandmother, who lived under the same roof. My sister was born when I was eighteen months, and my mother worked full time shortly after both births. Did I get what I needed?

The universe has thrown Julia and me together because we share something fundamental. We are both afraid. Can we find a way to comfort one another? We must.

Julia has a history of hurt we can't erase. She's been with us for three years and four months, but she subconsciously knows what it's like to slip permanently from her mother's arms. She understands the dizzying tumble from warmth and security. She remembers, no doubt, what it's like to lie in a crib and wonder who, if anyone, will attend to her needs and when? Then, one February day, a man and a woman showed up, put her in a yellow snowsuit, spirited her away in the dark night in a car, and then took her on something called a plane. As an infant, the guttural sounds of Russian filled her ears; at eight months, English replaced those familiar sounds. Briefly she lived in a glittery palace—a hotel—and then she went on another plane and was brought to a strange apartment. And there she met a cat and was placed in crisp sheets under a soft yellow blanket in a crib and stared up at a carousel of animals that were put there to delight her. Although these people who took her away had the very best intentions and thought this little child must realize how lucky she is to have escaped life in an orphanage, she must have been lying in that unfamiliar crib contemplating, *What will happen next?* This inexplicable change must have felt more like loss than luck.

Julia knows she's dependent on these strangers with their unfamiliar hands and foreign sounds and odd smells to feed her and change her diaper. She tolerates it, subconsciously waiting for something she remembers in her heart to return to her. And it doesn't. Over time, indifference morphs into anger. Her resolve hardens. *I won't let you love me. I won't love you.* At four, she's a vessel of resentment, seething because I deign to call myself her mother.

∞∞∞

Ricky and I are on a date night, which over the past four Fridays has come to be known as "data night." Instead of catching a film, we are returning to another bookstore. Ricky thinks we've found everything there is. In a sneaky effort to learn more, I've even called a couple of therapists under the guise of being a journalist working on a story. Reams of printed paper have poured from our groaning printer and filled every inch of my office. We've borrowed library books, too. We've gone to independent booksellers and this, our fourth Barnes & Noble, within a ten-mile radius of our house, is the last frontier, in case I've missed anything. Day and night, we share opinions about what experts say, we read aloud to one another, volley e-mails during the workday, and go to bed talking about our Holy Grail. We are certain Julia embodies the essence of everything we have read. We have a guide.

There is a lot of advice for raising kids with RAD. Some of it seems extreme—and controversial. Something called "holding therapy," which forces children who resist intimacy to be held against their will, seems wrong. Instead, we're focused on parenting techniques that anyone would agree seem counterintuitive. Imagine having to say to your child, "I know it's scary to love Mommy. But Mommy loves you and she always will." Not something most birth mothers ever think to say to their kids. The basic idea behind the parenting techniques is to "rewire" the child's mind. When you shift, they do too, the theory goes. For example, children like Julia don't feel punished during a time-out—they are relieved. It vindicates their belief that they are alone in this world. Being alone is a RAD child's best solace. It gives them the emotional space they crave. Instead of reprimanding the child with time-outs that send them to their room or isolate them, the books say to do the exact opposite. Give them "time-ins." Keep them close. Force them to communicate. Keep the bond solid, even if you are mad and the child is unglued.

Many marriages have been crushed under the weight of raising a child with RAD. This is one thing I don't fear. I suspect "Operation Love," as I call it, will bring me and Ricky closer, as every crisis has.

We are committed to pulling Julia from the brink. We will ground her. Attach her. Attach to her.

Ricky holds the glass door open, and I walk into the bookstore. He follows behind me.

"Let's ask at information."

"Hi," I say to the pasty-faced man with dark-frame glasses. "Can you help us?"

"I'll try," he says with a forced smile.

"I'm looking for books on Reactive Attachment Disorder."

He looks at me blankly.

I feel like I'm seventeen years old and I've gone to a pharmacy with my young boyfriend and asked for a pack of condoms.

"Shall I spell it for you?" I ask. "R-E-A-C-T-I-V-E. Attachment, A-T-T."

"I got it," he says, muttering the words under his breath as he types them into his computer. He waits a moment and then squints at the screen. Looking up at me he asks, "Do you have a title, an author?"

"No, I'm just looking for any book on the topic."

He resumes typing. The glow of the screen makes him seem ghostly.

"Not finding anything specific," he says. "I'd suggest you look at books on adoption and fostering. They're over there," he adds, pointing a bony finger toward the back.

Ricky and I weave through the aisles. We stop in front of the shelf.

"I'll start from the top; you start from the bottom," he says. "I'd be surprised if we find anything we haven't seen already."

"You're probably right, but we haven't been to this Barnes & Noble. I want to make sure we haven't missed anything. This is the last one, I promise."

An hour in, we're sitting on the floor in a fortress of books. We're thumbing through, reading bits to each other. Nothing new reveals itself.

Ricky looks tired.

"Is there still time to catch a bite?" he asks.

I glance up at the clock. It's almost 9:00 PM.

"I'd have to call Alison and ask her to stay a while longer."

"Do that," Ricky says. "We can talk about this over dinner."

∞∞∞

We are sitting in the window of an Italian bistro in Nyack. A clutch of teens populates the steps of a church. Couples amble by slowly, enjoying the sultry night.

"So what do you think we should do?" I ask.

"Like I've said, I think we should spend a few months applying what we've learned."

"And then?"

"And then, if we still feel lost and hopeless, we can seek professional help. I think she's very young, too young for counseling. Besides, I'm skeptical we'd find a therapist who has a real handle on children like this. And you know what else? I'm afraid that seeing a therapist will create a record that will follow Julia through life. Let's give it some time, now that we have a whole new understanding of the situation."

"I completely agree," I say. "I mean, I know we're not therapists, but look at all the things we've done together. We've moved mountains before and we will again, right?"

I look up at him and he's smiling sweetly at me.

He covers my hands with his.

"It'll be okay," he says. "We've made a good start. We've got our heads around the problem. We will help her. And if we can't help her, we'll seek professional help."

∞∞∞

I wake with a jolt. I peer at the clock—5:55 AM. I groan. It's Sunday morning and Julia is in her room, across the hall, twelve feet from ours, throwing dominoes onto her hardwood floor. She's not playing with the dominoes; she's dropping them from her hands for maximum thumps. *Grenades!* We know this because this is what she does; it is what she has always done with whatever is her weapon of choice. She's got a well-honed routine. She rises at the crack of dawn. She puts on her light. She leaps from her bed and orchestrates a jarring cacophony of commotion. Not once—*not once*—in four years has Ricky or I gone into her room and nudged her from sleep, and not once have we been able to awake leisurely or lie in bed quietly.

I've become an ugly morning person. Julia's trained me to beg her for quiet, to beg repeatedly. To get angrier with each pleading. To boil by the time I toss off the covers and stomp into the bathroom and slam the door. She used to chase in after me and say she had to use the toilet before I'd sit down. One day I locked the door. I felt a pang of guilt. But she found another way to war with me. When I went into the bathroom, she flicked the light switch, which is on the outside wall of the bathroom, on and off a dozen times.

Today, when Ricky feels me stir, he wraps himself around me and whispers, "Remember, we're going to try something different to throw her off course."

"Okay," I reply, my body stiff with tension.

While Ricky and I speak in a hush, the noise from Julia's room halts. She knows we're talking and she strains to listen, as she always does. So we quiet ourselves. What will happen next? Ah, the LEGOs! She starts threading her hands through hundreds of plastic pieces in her big red LEGO box over and over. Her hands are a sieve, except she's not actually looking for a piece to build with. She's waiting for a reaction. Ricky and I look at one another. He puts his index finger over his lips to keep me from speaking.

Kids with RAD thrive on chaos. It is always Julia's goal to unhinge me. She thrills when my head is on fire. The more monstrous I am, the better. How satisfying it must be for her to inherently understand *she* controls me. At breakfast, I'm brooding and ornery. She sits at the table, slurping her cereal, as self-satisfied as a cat who has snatched a blue jay for breakfast.

Ricky and I will lie in bed until 6:45. We will not say a word. No fuel this morning. She'll be knocked off her game. The books say that if the parents become less predictable, there's a better chance of interrupting her wiring. She'll need more time to process. She won't act robotically, because there is no rote script for her to follow.

After ten minutes of smashing LEGO pieces in the box, there's stillness again. She's confused. Hmm, what next? Boom! She's banging keys on the electric keyboard with the volume cranked up.

It's hard to remain passive, but Ricky keeps me contained by rubbing my back. At 6:30 AM, Julia comes into our room and whines, "Why are you still in bed?"

Normally, I'd tell her to go back to her room. I'd be disgusted and she'd know it.

Today I am someone else.

"Good morning, Julia," I say with Mister Rogers' flourish.

She's disoriented.

"Daddy and I are having a lazy morning. Why don't you join us?" I ask, sing-songy. I gesture for her to come into our bed.

"No, thank you," she says, creasing her brow. She shoots us one more puzzled look and scampers back to her room.

"Okay," I say loudly. "We'll all have breakfast when I get up. That will be swell! I'll make pancakes."

She goes back to her room to decamp. There's quiet. She's likely scratching her head, wondering what stranger she has encountered this morning. I must say I feel more in control.

Wendy is a middle-aged woman with frosted hair and a firm handshake. She leads me to her desk and looks me in the eye when I talk.

"I'm looking for a better preschool for Julia," I say. "I'm unhappy with Palisades."

"Why's that?" she asks directly.

"For one, the atmosphere there is dingy and depressing," I say. "More important, I don't think they have the skills to handle Julia."

"Meaning?"

"Well, in fairness, I never sat down with the director and explained Julia's situation, but even so, my daughter was not thriving there."

"I understand," she says.

She waits for me to continue.

I spool out Julia's story, telling Wendy that Julia is adopted and she has a repertoire of odd social behavior. I'm terribly concerned about her socialization, I explain. I assure her Julia doesn't appear to have any learning or cognitive disabilities. In fact, everyone believes she's a very bright child. But she is not interested in other children, which is troubling. She may appear friendly and vivacious, but she doesn't engage in genuine interaction or connection. She's been in daycare since she was two and has been in many children's classes, and she never bonds. No one ever calls us to make a playdate. Ever.

I take a breath. Wendy's face is open and kind.

Then I tell her what I believe is most critical. Julia seeks out the weakest female teacher or authority figure and wraps that person around her deft fingers. What she really needs, I explain, is a disciplined environment where the teacher is nurturing but maintains distance and does not baby her.

"I get what you're saying," she says. "We have a few other international adoptions here. I understand your concerns.

"C'mon," she says, squeezing my arm. "Let me show you around."

We leave the small crook where her desk sits and she leads me through two light-filled classrooms. She points out hanging artwork and a nook for books and cubbies and a bathroom. Children bring lunch. I follow her outside. Wow! It's how a Fresh Air Fund city kid must feel when he arrives at an upstate camp. There are two in-ground swimming pools, swings, jungle gyms, sandboxes, and lots of room to run. There are grassy areas to sit in and a picnic table.

"This is awesome," I gush.

Wendy tells me about the summer program. Kids take swim lessons twice per day, and they spend most of the time outdoors, weather permitting.

My heart is a helium-filled balloon, wrestling to tear itself from my chest.

"I'll get you the application and a check by the end of the week."

"Great. Camp starts in two weeks." She hands me a bunch of forms and walks with me to the front door.

Shaking my hand, she says, "Don't worry. Julia will be happy here. And really, I've heard what you had to say."

I step gingerly into the parking lot. I get in the car and drive a mile up the hill to our home. I pull into the driveway, turn off the ignition, and lean back in the driver's seat. I snap open my cell phone.

"I'm switching Julia's preschool," I say. "That place around the corner, Playgarten. It's paradise."

"Great," Ricky says. "Let the wild rumpus begin!"

Twenty-three

The hulking Victorian house sits across from the railroad tracks in the shadows of tall trees. I park at the back and scramble up a skinny flight of stairs in the dimly lit hallway to the therapist's office. Neal is a lanky man, looming at six feet, with a bushy beard and a pile of dark hair.

"Tina?" he says with his head cocked and a tight smile, "Your mother's not here yet. Go on in and make yourself comfortable."

The high-ceiling wood-paneled room is musky and warm despite the humming air conditioner. Curtains are drawn, making it feel like a dreary March day rather than the searing July day that it is. Neal's walls are plastered with honorary degrees and baseball paraphernalia. Stacks of folders rise like accordions atop his worn desk, which is chiseled into threadbare carpet. Wall-to-ceiling bookcases overflow. *Wait till Rosalie sees this,* I think to myself with a silent chuckle. *Neal's office—my unassuming town—it's a far cry from the sophisticated Manhattan therapists we both have known.*

Three chairs have been arranged for the session. Two are situated close to one another; the third faces the other two. I slink into one of the paired chairs and pull my shirt away from my sopping skin. When my mother suggested she and I go into therapy a month ago, I'd barked, "Why, so we can rehash a decade's worth of anger?" But after she planted the seed, the idea of doing something to fix our broken relationship kept teasing me. *What if? Maybe it's the only solution left. Our last chance to find one another again. My mother's not going to live forever. What if something happened to me first? And Julia—depriving her of grandparents? What have I been thinking? Doesn't a child with an attachment disorder need family to love her, even if that family is dysfunctional?*

I took it as a sign from the universe that the timing of my mother's call was not coincidental. At the precise moment I was beginning to understand what it was like for Julia to cope with a traumatic break from her birth mother, I realized I was living with parallel pain. I knew what it was like to lose maternal love. My relationship with my mother, the relationship I always took for granted, confounds me. It unthreaded slowly at first, after my divorce. My mother and I had different ideas about how I should rebuild my life. We had never been at such extreme odds. We fought and accused one another of terrible things and equally showed our mutual disappointment. In the end, no matter how much of a hand I had in dissolving our love, I felt abandoned. My mother was no longer there for me, and I found myself mourning her. She was not dead, but she was dead to me.

Rosalie was everything to me when I was a child. Our bond strengthened as I went from my teen years to young adulthood. Even when I spread my wings and experimented with sex or smoking cigarettes, she cheered me on or caught me in a great big net of compassion. Either way, I couldn't lose because I knew that wherever I was, she was there too. She insinuated herself so deeply into me that I had trouble understanding the difference between me and her. It was stunning to watch something I presumed to be as solid as marble chip away.

Divorce had stripped away my privileges, my whole way of living. It horrified my mother, me going solo, seeking independence. She didn't trust it. She'd been taught that women couldn't take care of themselves, but I wasn't going to wait for Prince Charming to come to my rescue. I didn't want to be like her. Maybe that's what she understood deep down.

Maybe that's how I hurt her. Still, in the early years after my divorce, I believed she was there for me and always would be.

Letting go of my mother's love was a choice I made, and I guess I thought I could reverse it. Julia lost her mother's love before she even had a chance to know her. A mother's love can be replaced and repaired, but only if a clamped heart is willing to reopen and allow a second chance. Julia's heart has yet to decide whether it can open up, and if so, how much it can open. She'll never recover from that first love lost.

Julia suffers, though she's too young to understand why. Her unconscious yearning must be wrenching. I, at least, have my grudges or rationalizations to explain why I'm in pain. Like I said before, I don't think it's a random coincidence that Julia and I have been brought together by unseen forces. We are both afraid of mother-daughter intimacy because we know the stakes. Is it worth it to try again?

In early July, I decided to give therapy with my mother a shot.

Neal lingers on the landing. I hear my mother's lumbering footsteps clank up the stairs. Her breathing is labored. She is on time, which is unusual.

"Are you okay?" Neal yodels.

"I'm fine," my mother says.

"Your daughter's here. Please, please, come in. We'll get started."

I am startled to see how hunched my mother is when she enters the therapist's office. I haven't seen her in months.

"Hello, Tina," my mother says in a disingenuous sing-song.

"Hello Rosalie," I say, our eyes meeting. It's the only way we can touch. We have not physically embraced one another in years. "Find the place okay?"

"Your father drove me. He's gone to your town library to wait for me. Do I sit here?" she asks, gesturing to the chair close to me.

Neal nods, and she settles in.

Neal is eyeing us. What does our body language say? What does he already know? What have we already told him about us? He clears his throat. He stretches his long legs into the center of our circle, his large shoes cocked upward. I look at them to avoid my mother's eye.

"Mrs. Traster," he says, addressing my mother. "I had an initial conversation with your daughter on the phone. She's explained that the two of you have been at odds for many years, that there's been a lot of strife in your family, but there is a mutual desire to repair things, especially for the sake of your granddaughter, Julia."

He pauses, the way shrinks do, with a deep breath.

"Is that right?"

"Absolutely," she says. "I have barely seen my granddaughter in four years. She's a stranger to me and my husband."

"Okay," he says, turning to me.

"From our earlier conversation, you've expressed a desire to work on the relationship with your mother," he says. "Is that right?"

I nod, thinking about whether Julia even remembers Rosalie. And if she does, does she ponder what happened to her because she hasn't seen her in months? Did Rosalie simply disappear the way her mother did, the way adults seem to do all the time? I feel panicky. What if therapy works only in the short-term, and we introduce her again into Julia's life and then the bottom falls out? *Focus*, I tell myself.

"I want to hear from each of you, for just a few minutes, a summary to explain what you view as the heart of the problem. Tina, why don't you start?"

Heat flushes my face.

I look at Neal, not at my mother, while I explain my theories about why my mother and I have come apart. I tell him about the divorce, the disappointment we both felt toward one another, and how we've never recuperated because I have not felt emotionally supported.

I occasionally glance at my mother and I think and hope so completely with my whole bone marrow that she's hearing me for the first time in a decade.

My voice is unsteady, but I continue. I tell Neal how my mother has not been able to celebrate or relate to my choices, and therefore she has missed out on so much.

"Okay. That's a good beginning. Mrs. Traster. Your turn. Why are you here?"

"I don't know where to begin. My daughter and I used to be best friends. My friends would always comment on this. They couldn't believe the relationship we had. Tina was a special child. My husband and I gave her every opportunity in the world: college, Europe, traveling. A beautiful wedding at Tavern on the Green."

I wince.

"We indulged her. Maybe too much. When she wanted to live in London, we supported her. When she and her husband—"

"Ex," I interject.

"When she and her *ex*-husband came back to New York, we set them up in an apartment. It's true we cared very much for her ex-husband and we were sad about the divorce. Who wouldn't be? But we *were* there for her."

I snort and Neal shoots me a look of disapproval.

"The thing is, after her divorce, she became very angry at us. Very angry and ungrateful. And very disrespectful. She blamed us for the failure of her marriage. There is nothing I can do about that. My husband and I are getting older. We don't know our grandchild. It's just a big mess," she says, blowing her nose into a tissue.

Neal returns his gaze to me. I'm lost in thought. I can sense that Rosalie wants a reconciliation; she wants to be Julia's grandmother. But I don't think we're ever going to resolve our true differences.

"Okay, ladies," Neal says. "This is a good start. Let's take a breath. It's good to be able to vent."

For what is left of the session, he keeps questions and answers clipped, guiding us as though we were on a footbridge over crocodile-infested waters. At the end of fifty minutes, he says he understands there is a lot of hurt between us, but if we are both motivated to heal the pain, it's not impossible. It will take time and discipline for my mother and me to find a new way to relate to one another, and the best thing we can do is to practice treating one another with civility and respect. He gives us exercises, including calling one another and making plans on neutral territory.

"If you'd like, we can schedule another appointment," he says.

My mother and I throw one another cryptic glances, but we agree to make a second appointment.

∞∞∞

The last of the catalpa leaves float to the ground. *Swish.* Sounds like an animal lurking in the brush. We're heating the house with firewood, heading into our second winter. The sun sinks early behind our mountain. I feel more peaceful than I have in a long time. My mother and I have been in therapy for four months. She and my father have seen Julia a handful of times. They bring her presents, and she looks forward to seeing them. I practice ways to be polite and noncombative with my mother, and she returns the efforts with civility. We're in a decent place.

I am sitting on the porch, wrapped in a fleece blanket, thumbing through holiday catalogs that show me what families are supposed to look like this time of year. I walk inside and punch her phone number into the keypad. "Would you and Dad like to come for Thanksgiving?" I ask.

"That would be delightful," she says.

"Okay, about 2:00 PM or so would be good," I respond.

∞∞∞

"Julia, come and help me," I say.

"What is it, Mommy?"

"Let's go outside and see if there are any colorful leaves on the ground and we'll use them to decorate the table."

Julia bolts out the door, but I catch the back of her shirt.

"Put on a jacket."

We gather a basketful of flaming red, golden, and burnt-orange leaves. The air is crisp and clean, the way Thanksgiving is supposed to be. When we come back inside, I tell Ricky to get the fire going. He is setting up the electric piano and a video camera.

"What time are they coming?" he asks.

"They're supposed to be here at 2:00. What time is it now?"

"I think it's about 1:15."

"Do we have the *Albuquerque Turkey* book ready to go?" I ask.

"It's right here."

Julia grabs it and starts singing at the top of her lungs, "Albuquerque is a turkey, and he's feathered and he's fine . . .!"

Ricky and I glance at one another with satisfaction. We've spent weeks teaching her the song about a turkey who's better thought of as a pet than a meal. Above and beyond a teachable moment on the benefits of being vegetarian, Ricky and I have accomplished something bigger. This is the first time she's let us teach her a long song without resistance. For weeks we've been practicing together, slowly picking apart the lyrics until she's gotten them all memorized. When she acted up, we didn't give up or show our frustration or concede defeat. During an early attempt, she flew into a fit, so we tried one of the new techniques we've learned. While she was screaming like a banshee, Ricky and I broke into exaggerated hyena-style laughter. We laughed hard and loud and harder and louder. It stopped Julia in her tracks. Instead of protesting the drills, she laughed with us. It reset her clock. We took it from the top, and slowly she absorbed the warm feeling of accomplishment.

"In fifteen minutes, we'll put on our costumes," I say.

"I want to put on my costume now, Mama. Now, now, now," Julia is chanting.

"Very soon," I say.

"No, right now."

I go back into the kitchen to finish laying the table, and Julia pads at my heels, tugging at me. I don't want her to spin out of control because I'm focused on setting a beautiful table, but I don't want to sour the festive mood Julia's in. Ricky hears the escalation of whining and he calls Julia into the living room.

"Let's rehearse one more time, and then Mama will take you upstairs and you can put on your costume."

"Albuquerque is a turkey, and he's feathered . . ."

I pull the gray, floor-length pilgrim's dress over her head. It has a scalloped white collar, white cuffs, and a white apron. I tie a white bonnet on her head. She races to the mirror and squeals with delight.

"I'm going to get dressed now too."

I wear a loose suede shirt, beads, and an Indian headdress. I braid my hair in two sections. I feel guilty about reducing Thanksgiving to the mythic Indians and Pilgrims cliché, but for now my attention is absorbed in healing two vital relationships.

Julia screams with excitement when she sees me, clapping her little hands.

She heads downstairs and bounces manically in front of the picture window until her grandparents' car pulls into our gravel driveway.

"They're here! They're here! I want to go outside and see them!"

Julia charges to the front door, but we don't worry she'll run outside and get hurt because we have the door bolt-locked at the top, way beyond her reach. She's furiously pulling at the knob, so Ricky leaps up, takes her by the hand, and walks with her outside to greet my parents.

"Look, look, they have presents for me!" Julia screams.

I watch this scene from inside the doorway. Rosalie has a big smile on her face. Julia has grabbed her hand.

"Happy Thanksgiving," my mother says, stepping into our warm house.

"Welcome," I say, taking their coats. "Welcome to our Pilgrim feast."

"Here, Grandma, put this on. Put this on. You too, Grandpa Tony."

Julia is handing my mother a bonnet, my father a conical pilgrim hat, white bibs, and shoe buckles.

My mother is delighted with dressing up. I can tell she already feels that we've gone to some length to make this day special.

"Come on, Grandma," Julia says. "We going to sing now."

"Julia," I say. "Let's offer the Pilgrims some nice spirits and cheese and crackers."

I duck into the kitchen to bring out a cheese platter. Ricky is behind me reaching for wine glasses.

"Where's Julia?" I ask.

"She's with your parents."

"Mommy, can we open presents?" Julia asks when I return to the living room.

"Let's do our concert first, okay?"

Ricky sits down on a stool next to the electronic piano, which is resting on a small table.

"Okay, Rosalie, Tony, we're all going to sing a song from the book that's in front of you, and I'm going to record it," Ricky says.

"One, two, three," Ricky adds, readying to play the notes.

"Albuquerque is a turkey, and he's feathered and he's fine . . ."

All the adults are singing, but Julia isn't. Instead, she's making silly faces and bending forward over the cheese and clowning around. She's deliberately baiting me, waiting for me to yell or become unhinged. Instead, I remain stoic and give her a couple of tight tugs, but it doesn't get her back on track. I know she knows these words cold. We sing through the whole song.

I don't know what my mother or my father are thinking. I have never discussed Julia's behavior issues with either one of them.

Ricky and I glance at each other. Nothing needs to be said. We both understand that we take a few steps forward with Julia and must expect a few backward. The road is not without obstacles, but still, I'd hoped that after a month of preparing, she'd be excited to show everyone what she'd learned.

"Okay," I say, gathering my strength. "Julia, why don't you open your presents, and then we will do the song again."

She's consumed with the wrapping paper and what is hiding inside the great big box. Slowly it is revealed. It's an American Girl doll. She lifts it up in the air and hugs it.

I'm surprised because I know these coveted creatures have a steep price tag.

"What do you say?" I ask Julia.

"Thank you," she squeaks.

"Give Grandma and Grandpa a hug."

Julia's idea of a hug is standing stiffly to be embraced and steeling herself for the unpleasant ritual.

I go back to the kitchen and return with smoked salmon blinis.

Ten minutes later I look at Ricky and say, "Shall we try it again?"

Ricky sits at the piano. My parents, good sports, put the songbook back on their lap.

I pull Julia next to me and clutch her arm with force.

I whisper to her, "This time you're going to show Grandma and Grandpa how good you can sing."

She gives a quick jerk, but I pull her back harder.

"One, two, three," Ricky says.

We start singing, and Julia is singing too. I've got her firmly contained, and she's not resisting. We've learned that RAD children subconsciously want to be reined in so long as the physical contact is not too overwhelming. Julia is now belting out the lyrics in a high-pitched, elated voice. My mother is smiling at her beatifically. My body is relaxing into the pleasure of the moment. Ricky wears a satisfied grin.

After the performance, Ricky fiddles with the VCR.

"Okay, I'm going to play it back."

And there it is. My dysfunctional family, dressed like pilgrims and Indians, wrapping paper scattered on the floor, singing a tune about a turkey that escapes being dinner. It's precious, an American original.

The rest of the evening sails smoothly. At one point my mother remarks, "She's an angel."

I smile and nod.

There was a time when my mother could read me like a book. The look in my eyes was enough for her to know how I felt, even what I was thinking. We've lost that connection, but I can sense that she desperately wants to get to know Julia, and for now, that's good enough.

At the end of the evening, Ricky, Julia, and I walk my parents to the door. Night has fallen. My father gives me a bear hug. I look at my mother; she looks back at me. We embrace awkwardly, but it is something. Really something, after all these years.

Twenty-four

I am on the down escalator, clutching Julia's hand tightly, heading to the children's department in Bloomingdale's. I have a flashback to the day she raced out of my sight, ran to the top of the down escalator in Barnes & Noble and nearly went tumbling to her death. The memory flashes in my brain like lightning. I tighten my grip as we thread our way through housewares to the racks of little dresses and adorable pant and shirt outfits. This is my maiden voyage with Julia to a store that was the temple of mother-daughter bonding during my childhood. This is literally the first time I am "going clothes shopping" with my daughter. Until now, I ordered from the Lands' End catalog. It was easy, affordable, and effortless—but it wasn't special. No emotional mother-daughter collateral in the bank. I resorted to catalog shopping because I was afraid to take her to a department store and chase her around and haggle with her over trying on one thing or another. I was worried I'd build up my hopes of re-creating something special only to be disappointed—or worse, angry. So when she was at school or sleeping, I'd open the catalog, dog-ear the pages, and order online.

"Look at these great clothes," I screech as we approach the little girls' section. Julia darts ahead—I release her hand with a bit of trepidation. She's circling the clothing racks maniacally, like a shark around a surfer.

"Julia, come here," I say firmly.

To my surprise, she rounds the corner and stands next to me, waiting for instructions.

"Okay, Mama's going to show you how you shop in a department store," I say, bending down to look at her at eye level. "First, we're going to choose a bunch of things that look nice for the spring. Then we're going to take them in the dressing room over there and we're going to try them on and see what fits and what looks pretty. Okay?"

"Okay, Mama," she says, calmly.

"Okay, let's find your size. Let's see, size four or six? Hmmm."

I receive a jolt of joy as my hand brushes through a selection of tiny sweet dresses hanging on little hangers.

"I like that one and that one and that one," Julia bleats indiscriminately.

"Hold on," I say, trying to combat the adrenaline. "Let's look at these carefully and decide what you really like."

It's not easy to pace Julia, but it's important to try. I take one dress at a time, hold it up against my chest, and say, "Look at this one. No, no. Really take a long look. Okay. Now do you really like it?"

I'm trying to teach my child to think about what she really thinks—or doesn't. Clothing can be an emotional decision. Shapes and colors speak to us. I want Julia to locate the flutter that comes from seeing something you really want rather than wanting everything you see.

Thirty minutes later, I've got a stack of dresses and cardigans and T-shirts and pants draped over my outstretched arms.

"Would you like some help with those, madam?" says a voice from somewhere behind me. I spin around and some of the clothes tumble to the floor.

Julia lets out a streak of laughter.

"That's okay," the woman says. "Let me help you with those. Follow me. You too, young lady. Let's go to the dressing room."

I'm surprised to see Julia in lockstep as we walk toward the dressing room.

I sit down on a cushioned chair and think about the circle of life. How many times did my mother and I disappear into a dressing room so I could try on the latest fashions? I remember times when we'd get loopy and giggly because we'd been in the airless department store too long and we were hungry, anticipating crepes at The Magic Pan. I can easily conjure the look of pleasure on her face while she watched me model tight bell-bottoms or peasant blouses. Once she cajoled me to try a skimpy, white knit bikini. It was totally impractical for swimming or even tanning, something Bo Derek might have barely had on emerging like a mermaid from the sea. "Go on," she'd said, with a glint in her eye. "It's sexy." I was fifteen.

"Julia, stop, calm down, come here." She's ripping clothes off the hangers and flinging each item on the floor. "Stop. Right now. These are not our clothes. We don't put them on the floor." I tug her toward me. "Take off your pants and shirt. We're going to try each piece of clothing on, one at a time."

Right at this moment, if she were a cartoon, there would be a calculus machine in each eye, sizing up her options. She's excited about the prospect of trying on clothes, that's for certain. But to get undressed without my having to press or beg her is to cooperate; it's a relinquishment of power and control. This, I understand, is a fork in the road. It always is. It's a juncture that causes her a feeling of unease, as it does for other children with Reactive Attachment Disorder. Here's how it goes in her unconscious mind: *Getting undressed and trying on clothes is exciting and leads to the prospect of getting things.* That's an endorphin release. Then there's the flip side: *If I cooperate and get along with Mom, then I leave myself open to feeling a moment of love and calm and that's dicey, because I know how ephemeral love can be.*

It is torture to watch her struggle with this every day over the simplest of things, over minutia. In a situation like this, we are alone, cloistered in a small dressing room. The stakes are high, and we both know it. I remain neutral while she shakes off her chaos, and I refuse to ask her to get undressed twice.

She dilly-dallies a few minutes, and then looks at me for a reaction. No dice. Then she kicks off her shoes, peels down her pants, and lifts off her shirt. She tries on one dress after another and then the coordinated little outfits. I can't speak because the lump in my throat has taken up residency, and no sound or sigh can slip around it. I'm overcome with the joy of seeing my pretty little girl trying on clothes.

Half an hour later, there is a sea of clothing on the bench in the dressing room. I want it all. Even more than she does. To make up for lost time?

Clothing is not yet important to Julia—it's more like something that is just always there, like oxygen. But I know Julia understands something special is happening here. Mommy is excited and super cheerful, which is not her usual disposition. At the register, I swat away any thoughts about being excessive. *Why not?* I say to myself. *It's long overdue.* The saleswoman folds each item and flattens it into bags. When she's done, she hands me two big brown bags.

"Enjoy your clothes, honey," she says to Julia.

Julia looks up at me. "Thank you, Mommy."

"Use them in good health," I say, which is exactly what my mother used to say to me after we bagged our prey at the end of our shopping expeditions.

∞∞∞

It has been one year since Ricky and I turned our attention to healing Julia and ourselves. It hasn't been a perfect run, but we are far from where we began. The other night, after Julia was asleep, Ricky and I examined what's been accomplished and what hasn't. It's a tricky analysis because Julia drops certain aberrant behaviors and replaces them with new ones, albeit what we see now is not as dark as what we used to see. One of the worst—smearing the bathroom walls with feces—stopped six months ago, which was a great relief. It started a few months after we moved in to the new house. She would come out of the bathroom, always the powder room on the ground floor but never the upstairs bathroom, with a smirk on her face. It had taken a while to figure out what she was doing, but after a while she'd trained me to expect this aberrant behavior. At first I yelled a lot, got in her face, and asked her why she was doing this. A few times I had her clean it up. I would fantasize about pushing her face right up into it, though I never let myself go that far. But once we were more schooled in RAD kids, my husband and I made a pact not to react because we understood that was the chaos she was courting. We maintained poker faces to deny her the rise she was looking for. And so it stopped.

This is how it went with many of her intentionally provocative behaviors. So she doesn't purposely spill water at the table anymore. When I pick her up at preschool, she doesn't retreat under a desk or make me wait; she actually runs and greets me. Then she collects her lunch box and jacket. When I'm not feeling well, she's more apt to notice and bring me a stuffed animal from her room. Julia has always showed outstanding artistic ability. We've noticed she's drawing cartoons with a mother, father, and child. She's processing the notion of family and her place in it.

Her impulses to be oppositional and rebellious remain intact, however. A couple of months ago she shoplifted a flashlight from Eastern Mountain Sports. "I want this, Mommy," she'd said, holding up the little flashlight. "I want it. I want it." I had said no and asked her to return it to the shelf. When we got back to the car, she took it from her pocket and turned it on and off several times. I caught the self-satisfied expression on her face from my rearview and intentionally said nothing. When Ricky got home, we had a Julia conference, which is a part of our daily routine. We agreed it would be prudent to frighten her on this one. Saturday morning at breakfast, Ricky asked Julia to get the flashlight from her room. She hesitated because she didn't know where he was going with this. Again, the imaginary calculator spun in her profoundly deep brown eyes. She scrambled upstairs and came down a minute later. Although her room is always a tornado, she knew exactly where the treasure was hidden. She bounded back down the steps and held it up.

"Mama tells me she didn't buy that for you," Ricky said. "She says you took it and we didn't pay for it."

She was about to take off.

Calmly Ricky said, "Do not move." Because he said it so sternly but without emotion, she froze.

"We're going to go back to the store, and you're going to tell the salesman you stole this and you're very sorry and you will never do it again. And hopefully he won't call the—"

Julia burst into tears. Real, hysterical tears. It surprised us because historically she is steely when being reprimanded.

"I don't want to. I don't want to. I'm sorry . . . I'm sorry. No, Mama. Don't make me."

What surprised us was that, literally, she cried like a baby. The kind of wailing that comes from a primal place. The kind of crying we never ever see or hear from Julia. She has an innate but unhealthy ability to resist the urge to express pain. But not at that moment. What a triumph it was! We both knew something magnificent had been accomplished, more than we could have expected.

Still crying, she collapsed into Ricky's arms.

"Okay, I tell you what. I'll give you a pass this time," Ricky said. "But if you ever steal again, we're going to go directly to the police station."

By now the tears had subsided, and Ricky and I felt pleased. Something mattered enough to touch her.

For the first year of our grand experiment in managing RAD, there were more bad days than good days. Ricky and I held each other up with encouragement. We'd pick out the tiny victories and recount that winning the battles was the way to win the war. There were times when I felt hopeless and wondered if we should seek counseling. Because kids with Reactive Attachment Disorder are detached, I had read that they tend to become more destructive as they age. They can be a danger to themselves, their parents, siblings, the animals they live with. I've read they hurt and kill animals, start fires, are sexually promiscuous, and steal. Although many have bright minds, they're too distracted to use them productively. I've read about parents locking children in bedrooms or stowing away knives and sharp objects in the kitchen. There are too many terrible stories about violent kids ending up in juvenile delinquent facilities and several accounts of parents giving up and relinquishing custody of teens or older children.

∞∞∞

One day I learned about the Ranch for Kids in Montana. This is a temporary home on a working ranch with horses and cows, in the aptly named town of Eureka, for adopted children who struggle with Reactive Attachment Disorder, prenatal exposure to drugs and alcohol, or other issues that make post-adoption life impossible and unbearable. For parents, this is the last resort for children they can't manage, though the price tag is nearly as hefty as a boarding school. The home, on 170 acres in the Rocky Mountains, is run by Joyce E. Sterkel, who adopted three Russian children, including a boy who had attachment issues. Sterkel, a midwife, had spent time in Russia delivering babies in the early 1990s. She knows a lot about orphanages and the way Russian babies start their lives. In 1999, after raising her own children, other parents of Russian adoptees asked her for help. In 2003, Ranch for Kids, a nonprofit group, was born. The stories I've read say hundreds of adoptees, nearly all from Russia, have come here to live and heal by way of communing with nature and living in a group setting. Some return home. Others are readopted domestically. A small percentage age out and end up in the federal Job Corps program.

Knowing about Ranch for Kids should make me feel like there's an alternative, a last resort if things don't work out. But it doesn't. It fills me with dread and sadness, which serves to fire up my adrenaline and make every neuron in my body work harder and faster every hour of every day to make sure Julia is never so far gone and out of control that we feel as though we have no other choice but to have someone else raise her.

A year down the road, we have lots of eureka moments. We see the work and focus paying off. We know she'll never be free of demons, but now there are more good days than bad, the opposite of how things were six months ago. She's calmer. I don't often see that depraved look she gets in her eyes. She's more communicative, which I guess is partly because most children have a big language jump between four and five. It occurs to me that her ability to converse and express herself and understand what we are saying has been a big component to achieving success.

I smile when I see Julia lift and squeeze Alex, our smallest cat. "She's mine," she says, pressing her face in Alex's soft fur. Julia never showed any possessiveness or favoritism toward a teddy bear or any one toy when she was younger, so this display of affection and the declaration that Alex is "mine" is a big deal.

∞∞∞

"I'm going to help Julia get dressed," I say to Ricky. "Can you feed the cats and get our breakfast ready?"

Today is the year-end concert at Playgarten.

"Hands up," I say, slipping one of the pretty dresses we bought in Bloomingdale's over her head and onto her stocky body. Then, I make two pigtail braids. I don't know whether to ask her if she knows the songs or whether to let the excitement of dressing up and looking special propel her. If I am overly assertive and communicate to her I want her to perform well, it will backfire. Unconsciously, the idea of making me proud of her generates angst, as it always does in her mind. If she succeeds, I'll love her more, and if she allows that, she could get hurt if that love goes away. I understand the counterintuitiveness of her psyche now, so on this occasion I play it cool. When I drop her at school at 8:15 AM, I say, "Daddy and I will be at your concert later. Good luck."

∞∞∞

Ricky and I are walking around the lake before Julia's concert. We hold hands and enjoy the silence. On one side of the lake, swans dip their heads like ladles in soup. Ducks congregate in the shallows. The path is not crowded, even though it's a perfect June day. As we round the bend, I notice in the corner of my eye a white flickering flash of a tail in the woods. I hear a rustle in the trees. Not fifteen feet from the well-trodden path, a doe nurses her spotted fawn. Mama's wide eyes flit back and forth furtively while her baby nourishes itself. I grab Ricky's arm and whisper, "Look, look at that." I gaze longingly. Tears trickle down my cheeks.

"What's wrong?" he asks.

"It's so beautiful," I say, shaking my head. "Natural."

I pause for a minute.

"You know, things are really so much better with Julia. The other day we were in the supermarket and when she called out 'Mama,' I noticed how hearing her call me that no longer seemed foreign . . . but still. I don't know. Look at how natural it is between this deer and her baby."

"I understand. I really do," he says, embracing me. "But it's not too late. She's coming around. She knows you're her mama. And she knows what that means."

I burrow into him.

"You think so?" I say.

"You know it," he says.

He's right. I do.

"Let's keep walking. We've got to be at the school by 11:30," I say.

Julia is always in the front row, on the end, at school concerts. She's the smallest one. It reinforces my fear of her being an outsider. Today she is on stage, bright-eyed, looking adorable, and singing the songs she's been taught. She's a little light on the hand movements, but she's humorously eyeing fellow students for cues. That she even cares is amazing. She's up there singing the songs. Progress. When it's over she flies into my arms and says, "Did I do good, Mommy?"

"Better than good," I say. "Awesome."

Twenty-five

Julia taps the school bus window with her balled-up fist and waves to me. She slides into the first seat on the right side so we can hold each other's gaze until the bus rolls past our driveway. Each day since kindergarten started three weeks ago, I choke on tears after the boxy bus morphs into a wisp of yellow streak and disappears. I hobble down our long path to the front door wondering what the hell is wrong with me. Julia's been in a school setting for three years, and I've never had trouble with the departure. I'm realizing you have to be bonded with someone to feel the wrench of separation.

There was a time when women with older or grown children would glance at Julia and then look at me with moist eyes and sigh, saying, "It goes so fast. Enjoy it." I'd smile and nod as though I empathized, but inside I'd be saying, *if only*. There were times when I felt like I had nothing but time, and time had nothing to offer me. Now I understand I have something to cherish. Maybe that's why I cry when the bus leaves. Or maybe I cry for the time when I didn't know this.

I met with Julia's kindergarten teacher before the school year started. I wanted her to know Julia's story so she would be prepared. I told her Julia was adopted and she did not bond easily. The early years were difficult. I credited Playgarten with doing a great job of evolving her and explained we were also working with her at home. I didn't delve too deeply into detail, and I certainly didn't want to bias the teacher or brand

Julia as a problem child, but I begged her to keep an eye out and let me know if she observed any kind of learning or behavioral issues. Before I left I said, "Just so you know, we have not told Julia she is adopted. We don't believe the time is right yet, so please understand, what I'm telling you is in strict confidence."

Each day at 3:30 PM Julia bounds off the bus, chatting her head off about her day, waving something in her hand. A drawing. A chart. She talks nonstop about Mrs. G. and the other teacher, who apparently gives her a lot of extra hugs. She tells me about circle time and how she's not really sleeping when the other kids are napping, but that's okay, "Right, Mommy?"

"Right, Julia," I say, "as long as you let the other kids sleep."

"I do, Mommy, and I pretend I'm sleeping too."

I'm sitting in a comfy chair in my home office, mindlessly stroking the silky coat of my newly adopted black-and-white cat. I should get back to my desk, but it's hypnotic to sit with him. He purrs like an engine, making my hand vibrate and allowing my mind to wander. Occasionally he lifts one side of his face and rubs it against my shoulder. We can't get enough of one another. He follows me around and I look for him when he's not by my side. We've only known each other for a few weeks, but I feel as though we've been together for a lifetime. It is that kind of love: unquestioning and profound. I fell for him easily and effortlessly, all heart, no head. He's the fifth cat to join our brood, but he attached himself to me like no other cat has done before. I didn't need weeks or months to prove I was trustworthy. He didn't test me or warm to me slowly. He allowed me to love him instantly, and I did. Patch, as I named him because of the patch of black fur on his white chin, attached himself the way a puppy does. You fall deliriously in love with a puppy the moment you lay eyes on him or drink in his smell. It is miraculous that a two-year-old cat who was discarded in a state park and left to die by some coldhearted human had room in his heart to trust again.

They say when you are ready to be a student, a teacher appears. This ten-pound feline has come to me for the divine purpose of showing me what instantaneous unconditional love looks like. He asks for love. I give it. I love him back; he knows it. The love deepens daily. This is what should have happened with Julia. But it didn't. It came when she was ready.

∞∞∞

I am driving Julia to a swim lesson. She's strapped in her car seat. As always she's talking nonstop. For safety's sake, I've learned to tune out her soliloquies because I'm afraid they will hypnotize me and I will slam into a tree. We're one block from the Y when she says, "What did I look like when I came out of your tummy, Mama?" I swerve the car as though I'm trying to avoid a deer in the road and straighten the wheel again, stunned and speechless. Julia repeats the question. After stammering I say, "Julia, do you have your bathing cap? Your flip-flops?" hoping to distract her, which is usually easy.

"You didn't answer me, Mommy," she says.

I glance into the rearview mirror and notice an intensity on her face I seldom see.

"Tell you what," I say. "Let me park the car. After your swim lesson, I will answer your question. Then we can go for cupcakes. How does that sound?"

"Good," she says.

This day had to come. All along, Ricky and I had decided we wouldn't tell Julia she was adopted until we thought she could process what that meant and when we felt she was in a good place to absorb that shock. As the years rolled by, we became more and more afraid of telling her because our bond with her had been so tenuous. After she started attaching, the last thing we wanted to do was to give her another reason to feel as though she didn't belong to us. Sometimes I'd wonder if she didn't instinctively know, but every time I played the soundtrack of the adoption talk either in my own head or with Ricky, neither one of us felt the time was right. In the meantime, we'd asked family members and old friends to keep it under wraps, and we hid it from new friends.

Years ago, when Ricky and I were first talking about adopting, a friend of mine told me about a friend of hers who had adopted two Russian girls. We drove to Philadelphia to visit them. They lived in a small house and welcomed us. The table was set. The house was quiet. The mother was preparing dinner, and the father chatted with Ricky and me on the couch in their tiny living room. He told us how he and his wife adopted a pair of young girls at the same time eight years ago. He had nothing but positive things to say about the process. While his wife was laying the salad bowl on the table, she called for the girls to come down.

All the adults were seated at the table. The two girls walked down the steps in unison and came into the dining room. They said hello and each said her name. Then in stereo they said, "We were born in Russia." One named the town where she was born, and then the other did. I was surprised they weren't wearing peasant costumes. We'd stumbled into some bizarre version of *The Sound of Music*. They were like marionettes, trained to perform the circumstances of their lives. It made the hair on my arms rise, and I wanted to get out of there as fast as we could.

After I drop Julia with the swim counselor, I run outside and flip open my phone. I'm hyperventilating.

"You are not going to believe what just happened," I say, repeating the question Julia put to me.

"What did you say?" he asks.

"I told her I'd answer the question after her swim lesson. What should I do?"

"What do you think?" he asks.

"I guess this is the time to answer her. Yes, no? Oh my God. We knew this day would come. What should I do? Should I wait for you?"

"No, no, you can handle it. Go on. I trust you. Call me later and tell me how it went," he says.

"Should I figure out a script and call you back? I have an hour; she's swimming," I ask.

"Don't be crazy. Just let whatever flows, flow naturally."

I pace the village streets for forty-five minutes, rehearsing lines in my mind. I could lie by omission. Worm my way around the question. I could say something like, "You didn't come out of my tummy. The stork brought you," and let it lie. No, that's all wrong. She's asking a question. She asked it twice. *Be brave. You can do this.* I'm afraid I'm going to lose ground. Now that I trust she loves me, I'm terrified to have anything rupture that fragile bond. I pace and pace, nearly oblivious to the woman I just nearly crashed into. "Sorry," I say. I am in a major life moment here, and I'm having a mini meltdown. I glance up at the large clock on the church. Fifteen minutes. I'm sweating. How do you explain to a child that one woman gave birth to her and another became her mother? Would it help if I showed her a few things we got in Russia? Her passport? *No, that's ridiculous.* What about the tiny baptismal cross that the orphanage caretaker pressed into my hand before we took her that night? It's upstairs, nestled on a soft tuft of cotton, in a plain white box in my bedside table.

Should I tell her while we're eating cupcakes, or should I tell her and then go for cupcakes?

Julia is padding toward me, dripping. She picks up her pace to a trot and I yell out, "Don't run! You'll fall." I take her into the dressing room and peel off the wet suit she's wearing. I towel her off. Her skin is cool from the water. I help her get a dress over her head.

"Did you have a nice swim lesson?" I ask.

"Are we going for cupcakes, Mommy?"

"Of course," I say, waiting for her to reprise The Question, but she doesn't.

"Let's walk over to the bakery."

We each choose a cupcake. I suggest we sit outside. Julia can barely hold off long enough to get outside. She's already engorged her face in it, and she's slathered with chocolate. I hand her napkins. Best to wait for the feasting to be over so I can get her full attention.

After we finish our cupcakes, we linger. It's a beautiful autumn day. Fallen leaves rustle in a corner where they've gathered. The sun is still hot.

"Julia, you asked me a question in the car before," I say.

"I did?" she says.

"You asked me what you looked like when you came out of my tummy."

She looks at me with no recollection of ever having uttered those words.

"Anyway, I want to answer that question, okay? You didn't exactly come out of *my* tummy. You see, I couldn't have a baby. And all I ever wanted was a baby girl. And there was this young girl all the way across the world in a place called Siberia who had a baby, but she couldn't take care of that baby."

I stop to take a breath. My voice is quivering.

"And that baby was you."

Julia creases her brow. She doesn't know what I mean.

"Remember, you had that book about Jesse and his adopted family," I say.

"Yes," she says, trying to connect dots.

"Well you have a similar story," I say. "I didn't actually push you from my tummy, but I was there to catch you when you fell into the world, and so was Daddy, and we are your parents now and forever."

Julia goes very quiet. I manage to prevent myself from going on and on. I've given her enough information to start with, and I wait patiently to see how she reacted.

"Is it like Patch? And all the cats? The way you've adopted them because they didn't have a home?" she finally asks, her eyes bright with curiosity.

"Yes, and no," I say. "No, I mean yes. Yes, we adopted you the way we've adopted our kittens. Wherever they had been living, or whatever their situation was, wasn't good. So we took them in and gave them a warm, loving home."

"I understand," she says, and I hug her.

I look at her face and hope she does. She's not visibly upset or shaken. I can't imagine what it's like to try to process the idea that the woman you've been calling Mommy all these years might not technically be your real mommy.

"Let's go for a stroll," I say, and she reaches for my hand.

As we start walking, I realize she doesn't have to understand the whole concept here and now. We have a whole lifetime together to make sense of this.

Epilogue

We are standing in an enormous circus tent on a one-hundred-degree July day. There aren't any free seats left in the bleachers. It is literally a three-ring circus here at French Woods sleepaway camp, with young campers performing acrobatics on mats and in the air. I've got the video camera ready to roll. I spot her, my brave daughter, dressed in a blue leotard and white tights, standing on a high platform and clutching a long wooden bar with two hands. She swings into the air like a tree monkey, and I swoon. Then she hoists her legs over the bar and dangles aloft, her head and arms hanging down. She floats through the air to another acrobat who catches her with waiting hands. Julia latches on and swings to a platform on the other side, where she lands victoriously. I am crying and hooting with joy. What an incredible leap of faith it is to trust that waiting hands will grab you and ferry you to safety. Even in this moment of utter exultation, I'm aware of what this means for my ten-year-old daughter. Flashback to the first time I put Julia in a baby swing in the park. She was frightened by the motion, by the feeling of being so out of control. For so long she was so afraid to trust anyone, really. But here, on this glorious day, I see how far my child has really come. To achieve this masterful act, she had to believe in her gut that others can be relied upon.

Moments like this, big ones, show me how far we've come. I am so proud of Julia and of my husband and myself. We've worked hard to put terra firma under Julia's feet, and doing so has allowed her to fly, literally. Very often I think about Torry Ann Hansen, a thirty-three-year-old Tennessee nurse who gave up on the Russian boy she adopted. In April 2010, Torry shocked the world after she put her seven-year-old boy, Atoyan, on a plane alone, returning him to Moscow with a note saying she didn't want to parent him any longer, that he was psychotic. The boy had been with Torry, who was a single mother, for only six months. When I heard the news, I was shocked, like everyone else. Although most of the world viewed her as a monster, I had an inkling of what it felt like to be a parent to a child who resists love. At this point, Julia and I were solidly attached, but the story sent chills up my spine because who's to say whether you can make love work or whether you can't? Torry may not have sought help, and returning a child as though he were a broken appliance is, by all accounts, wrong. Still, could I have ended up with a broken heart? No matter how hard my husband and I worked with Julia, we might not have had any success. When you've been on both sides of this equation, you know how fragile the line is. I can only pray that Julia understands I will always have my hands out, ready to clutch her, no matter how far the leap.

Conclusion

What Being Julia's Mother Has Taught Me, and Other Advice for Raising a Child with Reactive Attachment Disorder

I believe every adopted child, particularly children from Russia, Eastern Europe, and other international countries, is a "special needs" child. All have known profound loss at an early age. Most were denied prenatal care. Many carry forth a legacy of parental drug and alcohol use. Early life in an orphanage deeply influences their emotional and physical wiring. When we "rescue" them, we do so with so much love in our hearts. But love alone is not enough to undo their early disadvantages. Raising children with Reactive Attachment Disorder requires education, perseverance, patience, and an empathetic and informed community of people to embrace us.

Unless you live with and experience Reactive Attachment Disorder firsthand, it's impossible to understand what it's like. It's simply unfathomable that an infant could reject love and nurture. Adoptive parents raising RAD children will likely experience confusion, guilt, and possibly post-adoption depression before they begin to understand that it is the baby or toddler who is unreachable and that the child's inability to attach is not the parents' fault.

Anyone parenting a child with RAD—even those who were more prepared than I was—feels alone and judged. Ask one. Chances are they'll tell you, "Teachers, pediatricians, therapists, family, and friends did not understand what was going on. They couldn't relate. I felt totally alone." Since the early 1990s, sixty thousand Russian children have been adopted to American families. We all need to care about this.

I end my book when Julia is five years old—firmly attached by that time but always subject to the demons of Reactive Attachment Disorder. In my epilogue, I describe a scene that shows how far she's come, how she's able to trust. But from age five to forever, we will raise Julia with an understanding that Reactive Attachment Disorder needs to be addressed daily, often, and with focused attention. Looking back, I wish we'd intervened sooner. I feel blessed, however, because time has shown how effective intervention can be. My husband and I chose to work with Julia on our own. We threw everything into healing her. I am not necessarily advising other adoptive parents to follow our route. In many cases, professional help is necessary, especially if a child is violent or completely withdrawn. Julia's behaviors were never extreme enough to make us fear for our lives or hers. In contrast, the subtlety of her ways made it harder to figure out something was wrong.

Whether or not parents seek help, one piece of advice I have is to educate yourself on Reactive Attachment Disorder before you engage professionals. Put yourself in your child's shoes. Read everything out there. Ultimately, you are going to be your child's best expert and advocate.

My husband and I have and always will collaborate tirelessly to work with Julia. I can't stress enough the importance of having a good working relationship with your partner or support system. RAD children are experts at "divide and conquer." RAD children are proficient at creating chaos. Many marriages are crushed under the pressure of raising RAD children. I know a lot of RAD children who are being raised by divorced parents.

Somebody once told me, "Don't adopt a child if your life isn't already filled with love. You won't get the love you're seeking from a child unable to give it, at least for a very long time." I would not have understood this, nor believed this advice, before I brought Julia home. My marriage was filled with love, but Ricky and I wanted to round out our love by raising a child. I was prepared for the possibility that love between Julia and me might not be instantaneous, but I could never have guessed how much work and time it would take for us to be bonded, attached, in love.

Parenting a RAD child, even one who is attached and relatively adjusted and productive, is a slippery slope because you can never assume your child feels grounded and safe. One of the advantages of working with Julia when she was four to five years old was that we had the tools of language. For us, dialogue was and remains a key tool in keeping Julia attached and bonded. "I love you," is never enough, and maybe those words rang hollow for a long time. Always, we talk to Julia with plain, bold language. I tell her that I do the best I can. That I understand she might be angry at me because I'm not her "real" mother. RAD children need to be told the truth because they already know it at their core, though they don't necessarily understand it intellectually. I always tell Julia I'll never leave her, no matter what. No matter how hurt I am. I let her know it's okay to feel confused, even if she's not sure what she's confused about. I say these things often because I'd rather they be close to the surface than roiling around in a dark corner of her mind.

At the same time, I emphasize to Julia (as does everyone around her) how lucky she truly is. Lucky to have solid, happily married parents, good grandparents, excellent teachers at Valley Cottage Elementary (a shout-out here to Ms. Sue Goss and Ms. Pam Lima), a phenomenal sleepaway camp, and her own chickens! Julia also knows and trusts that I step in and advocate for her "just the right amount." I make sure her mentors and teachers understand who she is, but then I get out of the way and let them develop relationships with her. We stay involved, but we don't suffocate. This balance, I believe, is a sweet formula for a RAD child because it enables her to feel surrounded by unconditional love and support all the time.

Nothing terrifies a RAD child more than intimacy. Therein lies the challenge of parenting one, and of making sure he or she will have the skills needed to live a fulfilling life. A RAD child's basic instinct it to push away, recoil. How do we push back and gain trust? We used a combination of techniques over the years. First, I've never forced Julia into physical intimacy with me. I've shown her what it looks like by loving my husband and our five cats, but it has taken time for her to kiss me or wrap herself around me. I just had to be patient, and now there is no shortage of sloppy kisses or hugs.

We work tirelessly to get her to look us in the eye when she talks to us. Her eyes always wander. My husband always says, "Julia, I'm over here. Look me in the eye." This made her very uncomfortable. We did this for years, *years!* And now she no longer needs reminding. It's easier for her when we're in a noncombative situation, but as soon as there is controversy, she turns away. We work even harder to keep her focused but safe in heightened moments by diffusing tension as soon as it arises.

RAD children are very social in public. I always say "Julia works the room." Others always remark she's the "mayor of wherever." RAD children vie for tons of attention. People who know RAD children recognize their insatiable need to interact—but herein lies the rub. The so-called interaction is usually a one-way street. The RAD child wants to be in control, he or she is more interested in performing or manipulating than in truly relating. Conversation is often a monologue. Because we are so aware of this, we do not let Julia exist on a separate plane. We don't let her "entertain" us or take charge in a way where the end goal is manipulation or keeping herself at a distance. We work in a million ways to keep her at the center of things and to involve her in symbiotic relationships.

RAD children are reluctant to partake in ordinary tasks; they're not helpful by nature. In our household, we have not set up "monetary" rewards for doing basic tasks. The message we send is everyone lives here, so everyone participates. There's a lot of resistance, but we often warmly ask Julia, "Don't you want to be a family member?" Even something as simple as having her wait at dinner for everyone to begin eating emphasizes that she is part of something bigger than herself. It is exhausting to do this day in, day out, but I believe we must constantly teach her that she is an "us" as well as an "I."

ᴑᴑᴑᴑᴑᴑ

I crave order and routine. I would have been inclined to raise a child with structure anyway, but doing so for a RAD child is key. Julia came from an orphanage where she'd learned to sleep and feed on schedule. When we brought her home, we strictly maintained routines, and to this day, they serve to give our family an antidote to chaos and upheaval. Having strong-rooted regimens grounds Julia. She likes having a bedtime, even at ten years old. She likes fresh-squeezed orange juice every morning, without fail, practicing her violin in the afternoon, and knowing that every weekend I plan a special excursion. She likes knowing what to expect.

RAD children—and many are exceptionally bright—can really get in the way of themselves. A lot of mental time is wasted on emotional turmoil; concentration can be challenging. While their conscious brain is focused on a task at hand, for example, subconsciously there is a roiling undercurrent that pulls them in another direction. If a moment feels too warm and cuddly, they feel squirmy, uneasy. Feeling good can make them feel bad. Reliance on another person rattles them. RAD parents need to vigilantly watch for that sudden shift in mood. When you know what to watch for, you see it instantly. If these children feel a loss of control, they'll redirect positive energy in the wrong direction. When Julia acts up, we call her on it. We say, "Wouldn't it be better to use your energy to attract? Don't you think we'd pay more attention if you were saying something smart or doing something kind?" Over the years, she's absorbed the distinction, and sometimes when she's shifting and she hears these words, it's the "learned behavior around positive actions" that helps her rescue herself in that moment.

With RAD children, you need to remind them time and again about the same thing, but that's okay.

ᴑᴑᴑᴑᴑᴑ

From our earliest endeavors with overcoming RAD, one of the most basic tenets we've used has been to show Julia a steely, stony reaction when she's difficult and oppositional. We've long practiced responding to her in a composed, stoic, and steady way—most of the time. We're not perfect, but RAD children fish for a big reaction, and giving them one allows them to reel in the prize: chaos. Ricky and I speak to one another with our eyes when we're at the threshold of these episodes. We've learned to talk silently, to say, *The storm is coming. Prepare!* We've gotten good at this. Julia knows she's dealing with a united front and one that is pretty cool and calm. After millions of attempts at creating chaos have been thwarted, Julia has "learned" that life at home is not going to be a tornado.

You need to be aware of what is going on in the child's exterior and interior life as much as is possible—I suppose that's advice for any parent. I clean her room and her backpack constantly. I stay on top of all her affairs. I ask her questions all day long. I let her know I know what's going on. If I'm reading her correctly, and I think I am, it gives her tremendous pleasure to know someone's got her back, even if I'm annoying. I have the uncanny ability to know what she's thinking. Weirdly, that really thrills her, which I understand because I remember how comforting it was when I used to think my mother could read my thoughts.

Julia is entering middle school now. For three years, she's made an unwavering declaration: "When I grow up, I want to be a teacher for special-needs children." She'll make a very fine teacher one day. I can't even begin to account for what she's taught me.

Acknowledgments

The seeds for my memoir were first planted in essays I wrote about Reactive Attachment Disorder for the *New York Post*, *Adoptive Families Magazine*, *MaMaZina*, *Huffington Post*, and many mama blogs. I thank all those editors for letting me put on my training wheels and test my story. I'd like to express my deep gratitude to my agent, Linda Konner, who believed in my story from the start and who fought tirelessly to sell my book. After reading the first eight chapters, Linda said, "I don't have children, but this made me laugh and cry." My heartfelt thanks goes out to Lisa Reardon, my editor at Chicago Review Press, who believed I had an important story to tell and who had the vision to see the relevance of this topic long before the whole world began talking about Russian president Vladimir Putin's 2013 ban on allowing Americans to adopt Russian orphans. Thanks, too, are owed to all my writer friends along the way who've read pieces of my manuscript and especially to my friend and mentor, author Lynn Lauber, who has always been a guiding light. A special shout-out to Karen Gilbert, Julia's violin teacher, who reviewed the manuscript as an early reader and a constructive critic. My heart spills with gratitude for the adoptive parents who tell me their stories and who thank me for sharing mine in a public way. Finally, and most of all, I'd like to thank my husband, Rick Tannenbaum, who is my partner in every endeavor. Without his unerring support, input, and patience, this book would not have come to life.

Resources

ORGANIZATIONS THAT HELP WITH REACTIVE ATTACHMENT DISORDER

ATTACh
Association for Treatment and Training in the Attachment of Children
PO Box 19122
Minneapolis, MN 55419
Phone: (612) 861-4222
Fax: (612) 866-5499
Website: www.attach.org
E-mail: questions@attach.org

Attachment & Trauma Network, Inc.
PO Box 164
Jefferson, MD 21755
Phone: (888) 656-9806
Crisis hotline: (888) 656-9806
Website: www.attachmenttraumanetwork.com
E-mail: membership@attachtrauma.org

The Institute for Attachment and Child Development
5911 S. Middlefield Rd., Suite 103
Littleton, CO 80123
Phone: (303) 674-1910
Fax: (303) 670-3983
Website: www.instituteforattachment.org
E-mail: Forrest@instituteforattachment.org

radKIDS, Inc.
9 New Venture Dr., Unit 4
South Dennis, MA 02660
Phone: (508) 760-2080
Toll-free: (888) 482-1118
Fax: (508) 760-2089
Website: www.radkids.org
E-mail: radKIDS@radKIDS.org

Ranch for Kids
PO Box 790
Eureka, MT 59917
Phone: (406) 889-3106
Website: www.ranchforkids.org
E-mail: info@ranchforkids.org

PROFESSIONAL SERVICES

American Academy of Adoption Attorneys
PO Box 33053
Washington, DC 20033
Phone: (202) 832-2222
Website: www.adoptionattorneys.org
E-mail: info@adoptionattorneys.org

American Academy of Pediatrics
141 Northwest Point Blvd.
Elk Grove Village, IL 60007-1098
Phone: (847) 434-4000
Toll-free: (800) 433-9016
Fax: (847) 434-8000
Website: www.aap.org
E-mail: csc@aap.org

Attachment & Bonding Center of Ohio
12608 State Rd., Suite 1
Cleveland, OH 44133
Phone: (440) 230-1960
Fax: (440) 230-1965
Website: www.abcofohio.net

Center for Cognitive-Developmental Assessment & Remediation
Psychological Services for Internationally Adopted Children
Dr. Boris Gindis
13 S. Van Dyke Ave.
Airmont, NY 10901
Phone: (845) 533-4300
Website: www.bgcenter.com
E-mail: systemadministrator@bgcenter.com

Evan B. Donaldson Adoption Institute
120 East 38th St.
New York, NY 10016
Phone: (212) 925-4089
Fax: (775) 796-6592
Website: www.adoptioninstitute.org
E-mail: info@adoptioninstitute.org

Dr. Ronald S. Federici
9532 Liberia Ave., Suite 727
Manassas, VA 20110
Phone: (703) 830-6052
Website: www.drfederici.com
E-mail: drfederici@aol.com

International Adoption Clinic
University of Minnesota
Discovery Clinic
2450 Riverside Ave.
Minneapolis, MN 55454
Phone: (612) 624-1164
Fax: (612) 625-2920
Website: www.peds.umn.edu/iac/
E-mail: iac@umn.edu

International Pediatric Health Services, PLLC
Dr. Jane Aronson, FAAP
128 Maplewood Ave.
Maplewood, NJ 07040
Phone: (973) 763-3762
Fax: (973) 763-8640
Website: www.orphandoctor.com
E-mail: OrphanDoctor@gmail.com

TCU Institute of Child Development
2955 S. University Dr., Winton-Scott Hall #255
Fort Worth, TX 76109
Phone: (817) 257-7415
Website: www.child.tcu.edu/
E-mail: child@tcu.edu

GOVERNMENT AGENCIES

American Adoption Congress
1000 Connecticut Ave. NW, Suite 9
Washington, DC 20036
Phone: (202) 483-3399
Website: www.americanadoptioncongress.org

Intercounty Adoption Bureau of Consular Affairs
US Department of State
SA-29
2201 C St. NW
Washington, DC 20520
Phone: (888) 407-4747
Fax: (202) 736-9080
Website: www.adoption.state.gov
E-mail: AskCI@state.gov

Joint Council on International Children's Services
117 S. Saint Asaph St.
Alexandria, VA 22314-3119
Phone: (703) 535-8045
Fax: (703) 535-8049
Website: www.jointcouncil.org
E-mail: info@jointcouncil.org

ONLINE MAGAZINES AND WEBSITES ON ADOPTION

Adopting.com
Phone: (650) 493-7337
Website: www.adopting.com
E-mail: info@adopting.com

Adoption.com
1745 S. Alma School Rd., Suite 215
Mesa, AZ 85210
Phone: (480) 446-0500
Website: www.adoption.com
E-mail: info@adoption.com

***Adoption Today & Fostering Families Today* Magazines**
541 E. Garden Dr., Unit N
Windsor, CO 80550
Phone: (970) 686-7412
Fax: (970) 686-7412
Toll-free: 888-924-6736
Website: www.adoptinfo.net

***Adoption Voices* Magazine**
Website: www.adoptionvoicesmagazine.com
E-mail: ballback@cox.net

***Adoptive Families* Magazine**
39 W. 37th St., 15th Floor
New York, NY 10018
Phone: (646) 366-0830
Subscriptions: 800-372-3300
Fax: (646) 366-0842
Website: www.adoptivefamilies.com
Website: www.theadoptionguide.com
E-mail: community@adoptivefamilies.com

Attachment Disorder Site
Website: www.attachmentdisorder.net

Attachment.org
Nancy Thomas Parenting
PO Box 2812
Glenwood Springs, CO 81602
Phone: (970) 984-2222
Website: www.attachment.org
E-mail: shaye@attachment.org

Helpguide.org
Website: www.helpguide.org/mental/parenting_bonding_reactive_attachment_disorder.htm

RainbowKids
PO Box 202
Harvey, LA 70059
Website: www.rainbowkids.com
E-mail: martha@rainbowkids.com

Tapestry Books
PO Box 651
Ringoes, NJ 08551
Phone: (877) 266-5406
Fax: (609) 737-5951
Website: www.tapestrybooks.com
E-mail: info@tapestrybooks.com

SUPPORT AND ADVOCACY GROUPS

ARIA
Association for Research in International Adoption
University of Alabama, Birmingham
NB 320
Birmingham, AL 35293-1210
Phone: (205) 934-0630
Website: www.adoption-research.org
E-mail: teena@adoption-research.org

EEAC
Eastern European Adoption Coalition, Inc.
1075 Easton Ave., PMB 163
Somerset, NJ 08873
Phone: (732) 791-4606
Fax: (732) 791-4606
Website: www.eeadopt.org

FRUA
Families for Russian and Ukrainian Adoption
PO Box 2944
Merrifield, VA 22116
Phone: (703) 560-6184
Fax: (413) 480-8257
Website: www.frua.org
E-mail: info@frua.org

Index